SCOTNOTES
Number 41

Edwin Morgan's *Cyrano de Bergerac: a new verse translation*

John Corbett

Association for Scottish Literary Studies 2020

Published by
Association for Scottish Literary Studies
Scottish Literature
7 University Gardens
University of Glasgow
Glasgow G12 8QH
www.asls.org.uk

ASLS is a registered charity no. SC006535

First published 2020

Text © John Corbett
John Corbett is Professor of English at BNU-HKBU
United International College in Zhuhai, China.
He is also the author of the ASLS Scotnote on
Sir David Lyndsay's A Satire of the Three Estates.

All rights reserved. No part of this book may be
reproduced, stored in a retrieval system, or
transmitted in any form or means, electronic,
mechanical, photocopying, recording or otherwise,
without the prior permission of the
Association for Scottish Literary Studies.

A CIP catalogue for this title
is available from the British Library

ISBN 978-1-906841-44-7

CONTENTS

Page

1. Introduction   1

2. Summary of the Play   8

3. The Theatricality of *Cyrano*   23

4. Characters in the Play   28

5. Footing   33

6. *Cyrano* in Scots   37

7. Three Key Episodes   43
    i. The Flyting and Duel with Valvert   43
    ii. The Wooing of Roxane   48
    iii. The Death of Cyrano   52

8. 'A New Verse Translation'   55

9. Conclusion   60

10. Further Reading   62

11. Glossary   64

12. Appendix   81

SCOTNOTES

Study guides to major Scottish writers and literary texts

Produced by the Education Committee
of the Association for Scottish Literary Studies

Series Editors
Lorna Borrowman Smith
Ronald Renton

Editorial Board
Ronald Renton
(Convener, Education Committee, ASLS)
Gillin Anderson
Laurence Cavanagh
Professor John Corbett
Dr Emma Dymock
Dr Maureen Farrell
Dr Morna Fleming
Dr Simon Hall
Jean Hillhouse
John Hodgart
Bob Hume
Ann MacKinnon
Professor Alan Riach
Dr Gillian Sargent
Dr Cheryl Simpson
Lorna Borrowman Smith
Andrew Young

THE ASSOCIATION FOR SCOTTISH LITERARY STUDIES aims to promote the study, teaching and writing of Scottish literature, and to further the study of the languages of Scotland.

To these ends, the ASLS publishes works of Scottish literature; literary criticism and in-depth reviews of Scottish books in *Scottish Literary Review*; and scholarly studies of language in *Scottish Language*. It also publishes *New Writing Scotland*, an annual anthology of new poetry, drama and short fiction, in Scots, English and Gaelic. All these publications are available as a single 'package', in return for an annual subscription.

ASLS also produces a range of teaching materials covering Scottish language and literature for use in schools.

Enquiries should be sent to:

>ASLS
>Scottish Literature
>7 University Gardens
>University of Glasgow
>Glasgow G12 8QH
>
>Tel/fax +44 (0)141 330 5309
>e-mail **office@asls.org.uk**
>or visit our website at **www.asls.org.uk**

Brian Ferguson as Cyrano and Jessica Hardwick as Roxane, from the NTS/Royal Lyceum production of *Cyrano de Bergerac* at the Citizens Theatre in Glasgow, 2018. Photo © Mihaela Bodlovic. Reproduced by kind permission.

ACKNOWLEDGEMENTS

I am grateful to the ASLS Education Committee for the opportunity to write this Scotnote, and, in particular, to the encouragement of Lorna Smith and Ronnie Renton. Duncan Jones, as ever, has worked tirelessly in the production stage. I am particularly indebted, too, to James McGonigal for advice and his insights, and I'm grateful to Mihaela Bodlovic for allowing one of her publicity shots from the 2018 production to be reproduced. My own initial engagement with and gradual understanding of this play were enhanced by numerous conversations with the late Bill Findlay, himself a formidable scholar of Scottish theatre and a marvellous translator of drama into Scots. This modest guide is dedicated to his memory.

NOTE

The page numbers in this Scotnote refer to the edition of *Edmond Rostand's Cyrano de Bergerac: A New Verse Translation*, by Edwin Morgan (Manchester: Carcanet, 1992). An Appendix identifies some typos and errors in this edition. In his translation, Morgan conflates two of Rostand's characters, Cyrano's friends, Le Bret and Carbon, into one composite companion, Le Bret/Carbon.

1. INTRODUCTION

You are sitting amongst the audience in a darkened theatre, watching a play unfold on stage. At this point in the performance, you are experiencing a strange sense of *déjà vu*. If you have seen or read Shakespeare's *Romeo and Juliet* in any of its various forms, or even if you are familiar with the basic plot, you think you know what is going on: a beautiful, young woman, high up on a balcony, is being wooed by her new lover, who calls to her from the ground below. Such a portrayal of poetic seduction is now deeply embedded in our collective imagination – similar scenes have been recycled and parodied countless times in popular culture since at least Shakespeare's day. But there are problems with this particular scene in the play you are watching. First of all, all the characters, despite their period costume, are speaking in modern Scots, not Elizabethan English. More disturbingly, there are *two* young men under the woman's balcony, one hiding in the shadows and feeding his fellow lover the kind of romantic lines that the woman has insisted she longs to hear. So, you might reasonably ask yourself, who is the woman really in love with? Are her stronger feelings for the undeniably handsome man who is speaking the words, or for the second man, who hides, ashamed of his appearance, and who contents himself with supplying the first man with words that are so passionately lyrical that they must be sincerely meant? Will the woman be forced, later in the play, to choose between good looks and eloquence? How will this unusual love triangle work itself out? These are among the dramatic questions that drive Edmond Rostand's play, *Cyrano de Bergerac*, and its translation into contemporary Scots verse by the poet and dramatist, Edwin Morgan.

This Scotnote provides a brief introduction to one of the most important plays – certainly one of the most successful drama translations – in the late twentieth-century Scottish theatrical repertoire. It offers a succinct background to Edmond Rostand and his original play, which was first performed to enthusiastic acclaim in Paris in 1897, before it focuses on Edwin Morgan and his verse translation, which was premiered at the Eden Court Theatre in Inverness, in 1992. Morgan's version was later presented with considerable success at the Edinburgh Festival and in further tours and revivals, most recently, in 2018, by Glasgow's Citizens Theatre, in a co-production by the National Theatre of Scotland and the Royal Lyceum Theatre, Edinburgh. Rostand's *Cyrano de Bergerac*, indeed, is one of the most enduring and beloved plays of the past century and more, and it was and still is, repeatedly, revived, translated and adapted. It has been filmed numerous times, beginning with a 1923 silent spectacular, directed by Augusto Genina, that boasted a cast of five thousand, and there was an internationally acclaimed 1990 version, directed by Jean-Paul Rappeneau, starring Gerard Depardieu. Another film, *Roxanne* (1987), is a loose update of the story in a modern American setting; it was directed by Fred Schepisi and starred Steve Martin as the Cyrano figure, a fireman renamed 'C. D. Bales'. There have also been operas and a ballet based on the play. In 2019, the French comedy *Edmond* was released in cinemas: inspired by the Hollywood movie, *Shakespeare in Love*, it focuses on Rostand and fictionalises the writing and first production of *Cyrano*.

In choosing to translate *Cyrano de Bergerac* in 1992, then, Edwin Morgan was contributing to a near century-long tradition of translating, revisiting, refashioning and adapting a perennially popular story. In choosing to translate it into modern Scots, he was explicitly establishing a cultural bond between the classic French play and his own country's dramatic and literary heritage. This link was strengthened three years after Morgan's play, when A. L. Kennedy published *So I Am Glad* (1995), in which a female radio voice-over artist, living in today's Glasgow, is startled to find that she is sharing a flat with an equally confused Cyrano. Across a number of different media, Cyrano de Bergerac remains a vital and attractive figure in contemporary culture, in and beyond Scotland.

Edmond Rostand (1868–1918) was born in Marseille and studied in Paris. He began writing and publishing plays at the age of twenty and became known mainly for his comedies. None was overwhelmingly successful, until he produced *Cyrano de Bergerac* (1897), which benefited from the presence of one of the great French actors of the time, Benoît-Constant Coquelin, in the leading role. Rostand, in fact, dedicated the play to his lead actor. The play has always been a fantastic showcase for talented actors. The production was one of the most successful of its time, and Coquelin gave over four hundred performances in the role, even touring the play to North America. The play itself was quickly translated into many other languages, including German, Russian and English. The best-known English translations are by the American poet, William Brian Hooker, who translated it into blank verse in 1923, and by the British novelist, Anthony Burgess, who translated it in 1970. Burgess' translation was used as the basis for the subtitles in Rappeneu's 1990 film, which, again, was a perfect vehicle for Gerard Depardieu, one of France's most celebrated modern actors.

Rostand himself was inspired by the life and career of a real seventeenth-century French nobleman, Savinien de Cyrano de Bergerac (1619–1655), though the events of the play are largely fictional. The actual Cyrano de Bergerac was a writer whose life was documented in a memoir by his childhood friend, Henri Le Bret. Some of the 'facts' of Cyrano's life are disputed by scholars, but Rostand would have understood from Le

Bret's memoir, and the few other biographical sketches that were available to him, that Cyrano was from the rural French province of Gascony, that he was a minor nobleman who travelled to Paris to study in college, and that he then joined the Cadets, a branch of the army in which the youngest sons of aristocrats served as soldiers. He gained a reputation for his wit and boasting, as well as his prowess with a sword in duels. The disproportionate length of his nose did attract comment from his peers. He left military service to devote himself to literature, becoming a writer of plays and – most famously – fabulous tales featuring journeys to the moon and sun. Largely as a result of Cyrano's description of a primitive rocketship powered by fireworks, his tales are generally recognised as early examples of what we now call science fiction. These fantastic fables, on which the original Cyrano's fame now rests, and which are alluded to indirectly in the play, were published two years after his untimely death. Cyrano also had a cousin who married Baron Christian de Neuvillette, a fellow Cadet with whom, in 1640, Cyrano served at the Siege of Arras, one episode in a prolonged war between France and Spain. This cousin is the model for Roxane in the play, but, in real life, there is no evidence of any romantic interest between her and Cyrano. Indeed, it has been suggested that the real-life Cyrano was homosexual, and that his falling-out with one lover, the musician and comic poet, Charles Coypeau d'Assoucy, led to each ridiculing the other through verse satires. In the play, d'Assoucy is one of a number of literary contemporaries who are briefly named: he props up the bar in Act 1, Scene 2 and Cyrano seeks to avoid him.

Whatever the truth is behind the biographical fragments that were available to Rostand and to Morgan, it is clear that the playwright and translator were attracted to particular elements in the accounts of the life of this French nobleman. They were both enchanted by his gift for eloquent wit and fantastic tale-telling, and his reputation for bravado and swordplay. However, Rostand took elements from the biographical sketches and reworked them into a fictional plot that exaggerated the character's sense of shame at his physical appearance, and wove his self-loathing into a heterosexual love-triangle between the cousin, now named Roxane, and the two rivals for her affections: the witty, but ugly, Cyrano, and the good-looking, but dim, Christian. Morgan, himself gay, notes in the Introduction to his translation that the real-life Cyrano's alleged homosexuality 'could offer the theme of frustrated love an added resonance, scarcely but perhaps just audible in the play itself' (p. x). As we shall see, this 'resonance' is not one that Morgan insists upon in his version, but he is not otherwise averse to updating the play. References to the literary and cultural scene in seventeenth-century France and to Cyrano's own tales pepper both Rostand's original text and Morgan's translation, but Morgan gives himself the freedom to add anachronistic references to earlier and later twentieth-century popular culture, name-checking, for example, Rudolph Valentino, Gucci fashion, Rupert Murdoch and the action films of Sylvester Stallone. What we have in Morgan's version is a multi-layered text: he takes a nineteenth-century French play that is inspired by biographical fragments about a historical figure, a real-life seventeenth-century writer and soldier, and he reworks it for a contemporary Scottish audience, familiar with twentieth-century European and American popular culture.

Morgan's Scots translation of *Cyrano de Bergerac* was first staged in 1992, when the poet was in his early seventies. Born in 1920, Morgan was raised and educated in Glasgow. His university education was interrupted by his own service as a soldier in the Second World War. After completing his degree in English on his return to Glasgow, Morgan was offered a post as a lecturer in English Literature, and he remained at

Glasgow University until his retirement. His first published poetry appeared in the 1950s, but from the 1960s his productivity and reputation steadily grew. In 2004, his status as a national institution was acknowledged by the Scottish Government in his appointment as the first Scots Makar, or National Poet. He died, after a long illness, in 2010. As well as producing original poetry, Morgan translated the work of others throughout his literary career, from languages as diverse as Old English, Hungarian and Brazilian Portuguese, amongst many others. *Cyrano de Bergerac* was his first full foray into verse drama. It was commissioned by the Communicado Theatre Company, and, after premiering in Inverness, was performed at the 1992 Edinburgh Festival. Directed by Gerry Mulgrew, the play boasted a charismatic, swaggering performance in the title role by the actor Tom Mannion, with Sandy McDade as Roxane, and Kenneth Glanaan succeeding Gavin Marshall in the part of Christian. The 2018 revival by the Citizens Theatre for the National Theatre of Scotland and the Royal Lyceum was directed by Dominic Hill, and the parts of Cyrano, Roxane and Christian were played by Brian Ferguson, Jessica Hardwick and Scott Mackie. Morgan followed *Cyrano de Bergerac* with a new version of Christopher Marlowe's tragedy *Dr Faustus* (1999); a translation of Jean Racine's *Phèdre* (2000), which represented an attempt to write a full-blooded classical tragedy in Scots; an original drama, *A.D.: A Trilogy of Plays on the Life of Jesus* (2000); and a final translation, *The Play of Gilgamesh* (2005). Despite the poet's late flourishing as a playwright, Morgan's version of Rostand's play remains his dramatic masterpiece.

This Scotnote is organised as follows: a summary of the play is followed by a discussion of several fundamental characteristics of the play, for example, its overt theatricality. There is a general discussion of the characterisations in the play, and how the concept of 'footing' can help us understand the

Edwin Morgan's *Cyrano de Bergerac* 7

ways in which the characters in the play construct their public and private selves. Readers are invited to consider the translation's use of Scots, and there is a detailed breakdown of three key episodes (the flyting with Valvert, the wooing of Roxane, and Cyrano's confession and death). The discussion of the plot, characters, themes and the three key episodes includes a number of activities that are designed to engage readers actively and reflectively with the issues at stake in the play. Finally, there is a brief consideration of the relationship between Morgan's translation of *Cyrano* and Rostand's source text. The Scotnote also contains some suggestions for further reading, an extensive glossary that explains not only the Scots terms used in the play, but also some more obscure slang or technical terms, as well as Rostand's and Morgan's cultural references.

Activity

Find and watch one or more of the filmed versions of *Cyrano*, whether it is the relatively faithful historical drama starring Gerard Depardieu, or a looser, modernised adaptation, such as the film *Roxane* starring Steve Martin, or a film that takes a sideways glance at the play, e.g. Alexis Michelik's *Edmond*. Consider which aspects of the story transcend country and time – what is specific to France in the seventeenth and nineteenth centuries, and what parts of the story work well in twentieth-century America, and in the twenty-first century? If you were to adapt the story to a contemporary setting, in your own locality, how would you do it? What would you keep, and what would you cut?

2. SUMMARY OF THE PLAY

Act 1. A performance at the Hôtel de Bourgogne, Paris, 1640

The play opens with an audience gathering for a performance of a play, the tragicomedy, *Clorise* by Balthazar Baro, at the Hôtel de Bourgogne, a famous Parisian theatre. A Doorman attempts to restrict admission to paying customers only, but some people, like the members of the king's cavalry, claim free admittance. Other people arrive early, including a flower-girl and some audience members, and they pass their time fencing, playing cards, selling their wares, thieving and complaining about the dilapidated state of the theatre. There is a lot of cross-cutting banter till the arrival of candles signals that the play will soon be starting.

In Scene 2, the more socially notable members of the audience appear, just in time for the play to begin. They are the subject of gossip and passing remarks, in particular, Christian de Neuvillette, a handsome young nobleman who is about to enlist in the King's Guards, or Cadets. The audience is also impressed by the presence of members of the intellectual elite, the Academie Française, or French academy. Christian looks around for a woman who has captured his heart, but she is absent. He confides to a friend that he is anxious that she will disdain him as a simple, inarticulate soldier. The crowd greets the arrival of Ragueneau, a baker who is an ardent lover of poetry. Ragueneau is seeking his friend, Cyrano de Bergerac, who has threatened one of the lead actors, Montfleury, with violence if he dares to appear on stage in the role of Phaedo. Ragueneau describes Cyrano as a Cadet in the King's Guard, a fighter, a scientist, a musician, a man dressed in the height of fashion but cursed with a facial deformity, a greatly elongated nose. Meanwhile the object of Christian's affections arrives. She turns out to be Roxane, a literate, beautiful, young woman, and Cyrano's cousin. Her beauty has also attracted the attention of the married Count De Guiche, who wishes to see her wed to the Viscount of Valvert, who has promised the Count access to her after the marriage. Cyrano's friend, Lignière, has written a poem that exposes the Count's scheme. On learning of it, Christian storms off to seek the Count De Guiche, and his departure is noticed by Roxane, from her seat in the box.

Scene 3 sees the arrival at the theatre of De Guiche and Valvert. Christian is about to challenge De Guiche but he learns from an usherette that De Guiche has taken offence at Lignière's poem and plans to have a hundred men ambush him at one of the city gates, the Porte de Nesle, as he returns home. Christian reluctantly leaves De Guiche and Valvert in order to warn Lignière. The play, at last, begins and as soon as Montfleury takes the stage, Cyrano appears and challenges him. The actor perseveres, with the audience's encouragement.

In Scene 4, despite complaints from the audience, Cyrano continues to berate Montfleury. Cyrano draws his sword and threatens to take on all comers. Montfleury withdraws, and the audience and the owner of the theatre, Jodelet, turn on Cyrano. Cyrano responds by throwing the owner a purse full of enough money to recompense him and all the members of the audience. Unimpressed by this grand gesture, a Troublemaker continues to complain to Cyrano but is frightened off when Cyrano invites him to comment on his nose. Valvert, however, takes up this invitation, but his insult is weak, and its weakness is exposed by Cyrano himself, as, in a display of verbal fireworks, he extravagantly makes fun of his own nose, to show Valvert how it could be done. The two men then fence, while Cyrano simultaneously composes an impromptu *ballade*, a poem with a repeated refrain. He wounds Valvert just as the refrain predicts he will. The crowd cheers this performance and Cyrano is congratulated by D'Artagnan, the king's leading musketeer. As the satisfied crowd disperses, Cyrano casually admits that he has spent a month's food and maintenance on the grand gesture of recompensing Jodelet and the audience.

In Scene 5, Cyrano converses with another friend and fellow Cadet, Le Bret/Carbon. Le Bret/Carbon warns Cyrano that he is making too many powerful enemies. Cyrano reveals why he despises Montfleury – the actor dared to flirt with the object of Cyrano's hidden affections, his beautiful cousin, Roxane. Le Bret/Carbon urges Cyrano to reveal his love to Roxane but Cyrano is convinced his ugliness will repel her and he cannot bear the possibility of her rejection and mockery of him. At this point the Doorman, who is also Roxane's personal bodyguard, appears, and tells Cyrano that Roxane requests a meeting with him. Scene 6 is taken up with Cyrano's agreement to meet Roxane after Mass on the following day, at Ragueneau's bakery.

In Scene 7, as Cyrano celebrates the fact that his cousin wishes a rendezvous, he comes across Lignière, who admits to Cyrano that he is unable to return home because of the threatened ambush. Cyrano rejoices in the opportunity to face down a hundred men, and, accompanied by the theatre's actors and musicians, he heads to the Porte de Nesle alongside Lignière to brave the ambush.

Act 2: The Poets' Patisserie, Paris

The second act takes place in the Parisian bakery run by Ragueneau. As Scene 1 opens, Ragueneau is overseeing his cooks' efforts. He is delighted that one has baked a pie in the shape of a lyre, and rewards him, but his wife, Lisle, is less pleased. Ragueneau is horrified to find that she has been wrapping pies in paper bags that she has made from the pages of verse that his poet friends give him in payment for his wares. In Scene 2, two children enter the patisserie to buy pies.

Ragueneau cannot bear to part with the bags they are wrapped in and so barters for their return with extra pies. Scene 3 witnesses the early arrival of Cyrano for his meeting with Roxane. His hand is bandaged. As he waits, he borrows a quill pen and begins composing a letter to Roxane, revealing the extent of his feelings for her.

In Scene 4, as Cyrano writes his letter, the poets whom Ragueneau patronises enter and tell the baker of the outcome of the previous night's ambush. They claim that eight of Lignière's would-be attackers were killed by an unknown hero (Cyrano, over-hearing, corrects this number to seven). The poets admire Ragueneau's pastries, pies and cakes, and they listen politely as Ragueneau reads them a mediocre poem he has composed on the subject of a recipe for almond tartlets. The poets feign their admiration and Ragueneau admits to Cyrano that, while he is aware that his own poetry is considered poor, he enjoys reciting it and remains happy to support the starving writers. Cyrano is touched by this admission and demonstrates his affection for Ragueneau by warning off a good-looking musketeer who is flirting with Lisle. As Cyrano and the musketeer square up, the poets take their cakes and poetry to a safe corner to watch. However, in Scene 5, Roxane's bodyguard appears, and Cyrano bribes him with Ragueneu's poetry-wrapped pastries to make himself scarce.

In Scene 6, then, Cyrano manages to meet Roxane alone. She thanks him for facing up to Valvert the previous evening, and they begin to reminisce about their shared childhood. Roxane notices Cyrano's wounded hand and demands an explanation. Cyrano admits he has been in a fight, and Roxane tends to the injury. Cyrano coaxes Roxane into a confession of love, only to realise, after a few moments of misunderstanding, that her love is not for him but for a new recruit to his regiment, namely, Christian. She admits to Cyrano that while she noticed Christian at the theatre, they have never spoken.

Cyrano asks her how she would feel if Christian turned out to be an inarticulate fool; she responds that she would die. Cyrano then asks why Roxane has requested a meeting with him, and she confesses that she has heard that Gascon regiments can be hard on new recruits who, like Christian, are outsiders, and so she wishes Cyrano to agree to protect him. Cyrano agrees to do so, and he silently keeps to himself, unsigned, the love letter he has just written.

In Scene 7, Ragueneau, Le Bret/Carbon and several Cadets enter to congratulate Cyrano on his victory in the previous evening's swordfight, while, outside, a celebrating crowd chants Cyrano's name. A number burst into the bakery to lionise him. A despondent Cyrano rejects their acclaim. Among the crowd is the Count De Guiche, who had organised the ambush, and he and Cyrano are introduced. De Guiche, impressed with the crowd's praise, offers Cyrano employment in his service, but Cyrano refuses. He then offers to show Cyrano's recent play to his uncle, the influential Cardinal Richelieu, but he comments that 'a verse or two' might have to be changed. Offended, Cyrano again rejects the offer. A Cadet enters with a collection of hats, trophies taken from De Guiche's thugs the evening before. Cyrano asks De Guiche if he wishes them returned, an insult that finally enrages De Guiche, who leaves issuing the erudite warning that if, like Don Quixote, Cyrano wishes to tilt at windmills, then he might end up thrown to the mud. Or to the stars, Cyrano retorts.

Le Bret/Carbon begins Scene 8 by chastising Cyrano for angering a potential patron, arguing that he should learn to compromise his principles. Cyrano responds with a lengthy speech defending his stance of proud autonomy. Le Bret/Carbon counters by inquiring if he feels an emotional need to make enemies. Cyrano retorts that he prefers sincerity to hypocrisy, but, when pressed further, he admits to taking pleasure in seeing his enemies humiliated. Le Bret/Carbon observes that while Cyrano might present a proud and bitter face to the world, privately he is suffering from Roxane's indifference to him.

In Scene 9, Christian, the object of Roxane's affections enters, and a Cadet urges Cyrano to impress the new recruit with the story of his exploits the night before. Meanwhile, the other Cadets quietly draw Christian aside and warn him not to mention Cyrano's nose. During the exchanges it becomes clear that Christian is not from the same regional background as the other Cadets. As Cyrano responds to the Cadets' entreaties, he finds his story continually being interrupted by Christian's provocative references to his nose. Knowing who the new recruit is, Cyrano is uncharacteristically restrained, but, at last, he can take no more, and he clears the room of everyone but Christian and himself. The Cadets exit with Ragueneu, fearing for Christian's safety.

Scene 10 begins with a reversal of expectations: instead of assaulting Christian, Cyrano embraces him and explains that he is Roxane's cousin. Christian asks if Roxane reciprocates his feelings for her, and Cyrano is guarded in his response. Christian apologises to Cyrano for his insolence, and Cyrano tells him that Roxane expects him to send her a letter. Christian laments his bashfulness with women, and his inability to articulate his feelings. Cyrano begins to devise a plan to win Roxane's heart with a combination of Christian's good looks and his own eloquence. Christian agrees but wonders why this plan should so excite Cyrano. Cyrano admits only that it would provide him with amusement. As Roxane expects a letter immediately, Cyrano hands Christian the unsigned love letter he composed earlier, telling the new recruit to pass it off as his own. Christian is hesitant but Cyrano assures him that it will serve his purpose, and so Christian hugs Cyrano and the plan is set in motion.

Scene 11 concludes Act 2: the Cadets cautiously re-enter the bakery and are astonished to find Cyrano and Christian so friendly. They conclude that Cyrano is no longer so touchy about references to his nose. A musketeer attempts a joke about it and Cyrano promptly floors him.

Act 3: Roxane's kiss. At Roxane's house in Paris.

As Scene 1 begins, we discover that Lisle, Ragueneau's wife, has run off with the musketeer she was flirting with in Act 2, Scene 4. Ragueneau is admitting his marital woes to Roxane's bodyguard as Roxane is getting ready to attend a literary seminar on the workings of the heart. Cyrano enters, accompanied by two musicians who, because of a bet, are following him around for the day. Cyrano asks Roxane if she continues to have strong feelings for Christian. She reaffirms her love, and, in particular, her admiration for Christian's eloquence, which, she observes, strangely comes and goes. But, as proof of Christian's wit, she quotes lines from his letters to her, which, the audience knows, were written by Cyrano. After first deriding the verses in the letters, Cyrano finally admits to their genius. The bodyguard enters to warn Roxane that De Guiche is arriving, and Cyrano leaves.

In Scene 2, De Guiche enters to inform Roxane that he has been appointed Colonel of the Cadets, and he is taking his regiment to war, to the Siege of Arras. Roxane is unbothered by De Guiche's absence but fears for the safety of Christian, and so she persuades De Guiche that a way to punish her cousin and his enemy, Cyrano, would be to be deny him the opportunity of martial glory by stationing Le Bret/Carbon's division in Paris. De Guiche adopts this idea enthusiastically, now assuming, wrongly, that Roxane is an ally and a potential lover. He exits, and Roxane instructs her bodyguard to keep her part in this arrangement a secret from Christian.

Scene 3 sees Cyrano making his way with Roxane to the seminar on the heart. Roxane expects Christian to be present too, and plans to test his ingenuity by requiring him to improvise a speech on the topic of love. She orders Cyrano not to reveal her scheme to Christian, as she does not wish to give him opportunity to prepare his response. On cue, Christian appears.

In Scene 4, contrary to Roxane's instructions, Cyrano leads Christian aside, tells him of Roxane's plans and offers to coach him back at their quarters. Christian responds that he has had enough of mouthing another's phrases, and affirms that he has sufficient confidence now to speak for himself. Cyrano leaves him. In Scene 5, Roxane demands that Christian express his love for her. Christian does so, but in banal and clichéd terms. Roxane is disappointed and angry, and takes her leave, just as Cyrano reappears.

Scene 6 sees Christian distraught. He pleads for Cyrano to help him make things up with Roxane immediately. They post lookouts on the corner of the street where she lives, and throw pebbles at the window of her room, which gives onto a balcony. In Scene 7, Roxane appears on her balcony, and Christian, prompted by Cyrano, who is hidden in the shadows, woos her with Cyrano's words. But his voice is hesitant and nervous, so Cyrano, still hidden, takes over and speaks to her directly. Roxane voices her intent to descend to the street, but Cyrano persuades her to stay where she is as he unburdens his feelings towards her. As Cyrano continues to woo her in disguise, Christian interrupts, demanding a kiss from Roxane. Cyrano is discomfited but Roxane willingly agrees. As Christian and Cyrano argue between themselves, one of the lookouts whistles to alert them to the arrival of a Capuchin monk. Alarmed, Roxane disappears inside her room.

Scene 8 is taken up with Cyrano dealing briefly with the monk, who is seeking Roxane's residence. Cyrano misdirects him, and the monk passes on. Scene 9 sees Christian returning to the topic of Roxane's kiss: he persuades an understandably reluctant Cyrano to engineer the situation in his favour. In Scene 10, Roxane reappears on her balcony, and she also is keen to return to the topic of the kiss. To her frustration, Cyrano embarks on a witty speech on the nature of kisses, and he is carried away by his own eloquence until a remark by Roxane reminds him that he is actually speaking for Christian. Roxane instructs him to climb up to her, and after some persuasion by Cyrano, a nervous Christian joins her on the balcony. As Cyrano contemplates his mixed feelings below, he hears the lookouts whistling again to warn of the monk's return. He calls up to warn the lovers, and Roxane and Christian descend to street level.

In Scene 11, the monk informs Roxane, or Magdalene Robin, to give her her full name, that he is carrying a letter from De Guiche. Roxane takes the letter aside and reads it, realising that it is a request from De Guiche that she should dismiss her household staff so that she can meet him, shortly, in private. However, she tells the monk that the letter is in fact an order from Cardinal Richelieu via De Guiche to the effect that she must secretly marry Christian, and that the monk must perform the ceremony on the spot. When Roxane adds that the monastery will receive a handsome donation, the monk is delighted to comply, and so he, Roxane and Christian re-enter the house. Cyrano waits outside in order to detain De Guiche for the ten minutes necessary for the marriage to take place. Scene 12 sees Cyrano climbing up to Roxane's balcony, as he ponders how best to distract De Guiche when he arrives.

In Scene 13, De Guiche arrives, masked and wondering where the monk has got to. Cyrano also covers his face, and, changing the timbre of his voice, he tumbles from the balcony to street level, to inform De Guiche that he has fallen all the way from the moon. De Guiche thinks that the stranger is mad but decides to humour him. Cyrano tells a fantastic tale of his cosmic journey and, despite his urgent desire to see Roxane, De Guiche becomes fascinated by the inventiveness of Cyrano's tale, which includes an account of six different ways to reach the moon. When De Guiche asks which method Cyrano used, he devises a seventh, claiming that he lay wet in the sand after a dip in the ocean, and let the moon draw him up with the tide. Intrigued, De Guiche asks what happened next – but the ten minutes are up, and Cyrano reveals his identity and informs De Guiche that Roxane and Christian are wed. The couple appears.

Scene 14 witnesses De Guiche's fury. He nevertheless compliments Cyrano on his tale, observing that it would make a fine book. He then orders Roxane to bid her new husband farewell, as he is rescinding his previous order and sending Christian and Cyrano's regiment of Cadets directly to the war. Roxane again pleads with Cyrano to protect Christian, and makes him promise that Christian will write to her. Cyrano is happy to promise the latter.

Act 4: The Gascon Cadets at the Siege of Arras.

The first scene in the fourth act finds the Cadets starving and surrounded by hostile Spanish troops. Despite the danger, Cyrano risks his life, every morning and evening, by crossing the enemy lines to send letters to Roxane. In Scene 2 the Cadets waken at reveille after dreaming of food. Le Bret/Carbon asks Cyrano to distract them from their hunger. Scene 3 is taken up with Cyrano's response to his friend's request: to each Cadet's complaint he gives a witty response, before playing music from their Gascon homeland to help them forget their hunger. As the soldiers weep with homesickness, Le Bret/Carbon complains to Cyrano that he is making them too soft for battle. Cyrano orders a drum roll and the Cadets immediately demonstrate their readiness to fight. De Guiche arrives, and the Cadets feign nonchalance about their suffering.

In Scene 4 De Guiche boasts of his exploits in a recent battle. He tells the story of charging the Spanish and finding himself stranded across enemy lines. He would have been recognised, captured, and perhaps executed had he not had the foresight to relinquish the white scarf that was his badge of rank. Unimpressed, Cyrano scolds De Guiche for losing this symbol of honour, and, in a flourish, shows that he, himself, has recovered it. De Guiche is nonplussed, and goes on to say that the French Marshal has temporarily withdrawn a substantial number of troops. De Guiche's spy in the Spanish camp has informed him that the Spanish are aware of the French troops' current weakness, and so De Guiche requires a regiment to take on the suicide mission of defending the French lines until the Marshal's return. For this, he has chosen the Gascon Cadets. Cyrano thanks De Guiche for this opportunity to show the Cadets' courage. Christian laments the lack of opportunity even to write a farewell letter to Roxane; Cyrano shows him one he has already composed. Christian begins to read Cyrano's letter, at which point a carriage unexpectedly arrives – and Roxane steps out.

Scene 5 is taken up with Roxane's story of how, to the astonishment of the listening Cadets, she passed safely through the Spanish lines by smiling at the enemy troops and informing them she was travelling on a romantic mission to meet her lover. The soldiers implore her to leave, but she insists on remaining and if necessary dying with her husband. In Scene 6 the Cadets make it clear to Roxane that they are troops fated to perish. They take her lace handkerchief as their banner. Roxane orders a fine meal for herself, and, when the Cadets inform her that they are in fact starving, she reveals that her coachman is Ragueneau, the pastry chef, and that her carriage is packed with delicacies. As the men tuck in to a surprise banquet, Cyrano tries unsuccessfully to engage Christian in conversation. And then De Guiche returns from inspecting the cannon, and the Cadets quickly hide the food.

Scene 7 sees De Guiche surprised to find the Cadets so happy. Discovering Roxane's presence, he tries to persuade her to flee. As he is unsuccessful in changing her mind, he resolves, himself, to remain and fight to the death with the Cadets. Cyrano commends him on his courage. Christian asks Cyrano why he wished to speak to him and Cyrano explains that Roxane has received more letters from him than he might have imagined. He admits that he has been braving the enemy lines twice a day to send them. Roxane interrupts this conversation, and in Scene 8 she takes Christian aside to tell him how much she adored his letters. She confesses to once loving him only for his beauty, but now acknowledges that, thanks to his letters, she loves him for his soul alone. She goes so far as to insist that if he ever lost his good looks she would still love him as dearly. Christian does not know how to respond, and so he takes her back to inspect the Cadets before battle.

In Scene 9 Christian confronts Cyrano and tells him of Roxane's admission, informing Cyrano that he is the true recipient of Roxane's love. Cyrano admits that he, himself, is also in love with Roxane; however, he continues to insist that she could never love someone as ugly as he is. Christian refutes this, and demands that they confess everything to Roxane and let her choose between them. He calls Roxane and leaves her alone with Cyrano.

In Scene 10 Roxane repeats to Cyrano her strong affirmation that she would love Christian, even if he were ugly. Cyrano, encouraged, is about to confess to being the author of all the letters, when Le Bret/Carbon enters with the news that Christian has been fatally wounded in battle. Cyrano and Roxane rush to him, and, before he dies, Cyrano quietly lies to him that he has informed Roxane of their deception, and that Roxane has chosen Christian over himself. Christian dies, and Roxane embraces his body, his blood smearing the letters. Cyrano advises De Guiche to flee with Roxane and Ragueneau, while he and the rest of the Cadets fight the advancing Spanish.

Act 5: The park of the convent of the Ladies of the Cross, Paris, fifteen years later, 1655.

As Scene 1 opens, fifteen years have passed since the Siege of Arras, and it is the autumn of 1655. In a convent, two nuns gossip with the Mother Superior, their conversation turning on the weekly visit of Cyrano to the widow, Roxane, who now lives amongst them, in mourning. Cyrano's visits are a regular source of amusement to the nuns, whom he scandalises with his irreverent humour. For example, he claims to eat meat on Fridays, though the Mother Superior knows that, in reality, he lives in poverty and hunger. The nuns depart, leaving the stage to Roxane and her occasional visitor, De Guiche, who is now a Duke. In Scene 2 De Guiche asks for Roxane's forgiveness for his past behaviour, and asks if she still keeps Christian's last, bloodstained letter close to her heart. Roxane confirms that she does. Le Bret/Carbon enters and informs the pair that Cyrano is now friendless, alone and starving, and his satirical writing is earning him only enemies. De Guiche observes that Cyrano has always been an independent free-thinker, and looks back with regret at the compromises he himself has made as he has ascended in society. As he leaves, he informs Le Bret/Carbon in an aside that he has heard a rumour that Cyrano will be attacked, and that he should be warned to stay at home. A nun announces the arrival of Ragueneau, and in Scene 3, the pastry chef converses with Le Bret/Carbon alone. Ragueneau tells him that he had recently witnessed an assassin at a window, dropping a heavy log on Cyrano as he passed below. Ragueneau then took Cyrano to his home where a charity doctor attended to him, bandaging his injured head. Le Bret/Carbon hurries off to ensure Cyrano has company at his sick bed, and so, when Roxane reappears, she is surprised to find herself alone.

In Scene 4, Roxane observes to a nun that Cyrano is uncharacteristically late for his weekly visit. As she takes up some needlework, Cyrano's arrival is announced. Scene 5 begins with Roxane teasing Cyrano for being late. Cyrano is fatally wounded but hides this from Roxane; only the nuns realise how badly injured he is. Cyrano begins to recite to Roxane his regular weekly 'gazette', or account of the events of the past seven days. As he does so, he loses consciousness, but recovers quickly, blaming an old wound, received at the Siege of Arras. Roxane talks of her own emotional wounds, and of Christian's last letter to her, which Cyrano asks to read. Roxane gives it to him, and Cyrano begins to read the letter aloud. Roxane is impressed by the feeling he gives to his performance, and she gradually realises that the voice and the sentiments belong to the person who wooed her on her balcony. She also realises that darkness has fallen, and so Cyrano should be unable to see the words on the page. She confronts Cyrano with the fact that he is the author of the letters, but he denies this. She points to his tears on the letter, and, in response, he points to the traces of Christian's blood. Roxane asks why Cyrano has chosen to break his silence after so many years.

In Scene 6, which concludes the play, Ragueneau and Le Bret/Carbon re-enter and Roxane realises how badly Cyrano is wounded. Cyrano resumes his account of the week's events, concluding with the episode of his own murder. He removes his hat to reveal his bandaged head. Roxane calls the sisters for help, and, as Cyrano prepares for death, she declares her love for him, and begs him to live. She laments that she was the cause of his misery; Cyrano counters by affirming that hers is the only womanly affection he has ever enjoyed.

Weakening further, he again imagines himself being swept up to the moon, to meet fellow philosophers and scientists, Socrates and Galileo. He composes his own epitaph and asks Roxane to reserve some of her grief for him. Then he stands up, sword in hand, as he senses the approach of Death. As his life slips finally away, his old, thrawn spirit revives momentarily, and he prepares to give an extravagant bow at the gates of heaven, taking off his hat and flourishing its feathered plume.

3. THE THEATRICALITY OF *CYRANO*

From the summary of the play, it should be clear that one of the reasons for Cyrano's immediate and lasting popularity on stage and film is that it is itself a love letter to a particular kind of theatricality. As the curtain rises, the audience in the theatre (or cinema) enters another theatre, namely the Hôtel de Bourgogne in Paris, in 1640. The contemporary audience is drawn into the arrival of another, historical audience, made up of cavaliers, gamblers, flower girls, members of the bourgeoisie and intellectuals from the French academy, all excitedly anticipating a performance of *Clorise*, a play by the French dramatist Balthazar Baro. Another play, Corneille's *Le Cid (The Cid)* is mentioned in the first scene. The contemporary audience is thus assimilated into a historical performance at a key moment in the history of French drama, a period in the seventeenth century when there was a cultural shift from Baro's Classicism to Corneille's Romanticism. This shift in the nature of the dramatic medium was occurring just as the intellectuals of the French academy, who have come to the theatre to admire the older style of play, were drawing up regulations to govern theatrical conventions. Dramatists like Corneille, Racine and Molière were at the vanguard of a new generation of playwrights who resisted these theatrical conventions. The performance of *Clorise* promises, or rather threatens, to be in the old-fashioned Classical style, in which actors would generally assume static poses before the audience and declaim their profound but restrained feelings in a grand, rhetorical fashion. The eruption of Cyrano into this environment to halt the performance, banish the lead actor, and provide entertainment for the assembled crowd by combining an impromptu poetic composition with a fencing match, indirectly epitomises the new

Romantic spirit. Rather than a static, oratorical display of restrained feelings, we have, in Cyrano's duel, unrestrained but sympathetic emotion in action. His wit is presented as improvised rather than scripted, his eloquence is aroused by his genuine feelings, and he displays authentic bravado in the fencing match with Valvert. And yet, like Montfleury, he performs to the crowd, enjoying the grand gesture of scattering to the audience the money that would otherwise sustain him for a month, in order to compensate them for his disruption of the advertised play. From the first scene, then, we have the banishment of a Classical performance and the arrival of a new type of Romantic hero: a man whose principles, wit and bravado are driven by an unruly but deep-seated and authentic emotion.

Much of the action of *Cyrano* takes place in a web of literary and cultural allusions. The play is peppered with many names and references that, perhaps, educated members of the nineteenth-century French audience would have recognised, but which are less familiar, arguably, even to cultured Scottish audiences and readers in the twentieth and twenty-first centuries. We can think of these fleeting references to cultural icons as cameos in the extended universe in which Cyrano exists. D'Artagnan, the main character in Alexandre Dumas' *The Three Musketeers*, pops up to deliver a line; the powerful figure of Cardinal Richelieu is an uneasy presence in the background; and there are throwaway references to other major and minor literary figures like Molière, Corneille, Isaac de Benserade, and Jean de Rotrou. 'These names will live forever!' cry members of the enraptured audience onstage. The joke, of course, is that not all of them have, and the contemporary translator has to decide what to do about the many references to figures who are now forgotten. Perhaps we need simply enjoy the frequent mention of lesser-known characters simply as names, mellifluent in their Frenchness, like the polysyllabic names of Roxane's female friends, Barthénoïde, Urimédonte, Cassandace and Félixérie. But we also need to recognise that *Cyrano* is a work of literature that portrays a world that is defined by its cultural activities, and that the constant allusion to historical legends, and to dramatists, poets and visual artists, and their creations, is a continual reminder of the constructed nature of *Cyrano*'s universe. To a certain extent, Morgan as a translator chooses to update Rostand's strategy, also name-checking a number of iconic cultural figures and products of the early 1990s: Gucci, Rupert Murdoch, Rambo, and Emilio Coia. But he also retains a number of the original allusions. The most prominent of these references, modern as well as historical, are explained briefly in the Glossary (p. 64).

The themes of performance and culture extend to the object of Cyrano and Christian's affections, Roxane. A member of the theatre audience as the play opens, she is, as we later find out, a woman whose values and romantic expectations have been formed by attending plays, salons, lectures and readings, and so she demands to be wooed by eloquence and wit. In seventeenth-century Paris, she is one of a recognisable class of such women, who were called *précieuses*. As a *précieuse*, Roxane demands that her suitor match his feelings with appropriate words, that is to say, he must demonstrate his love for her in conversation by means of a lively and sophisticated verbal performance. Christian, whose good looks she is attracted to, cannot meet her expectations in this respect. Cyrano, who considers himself too ugly to win her, is an eloquent suitor, and so a love triangle is established whereby Cyrano secretly provides Christian with the wit and eloquence necessary to woo the woman they both love. Roxane, however, is not merely an audience for their performance, nor is she simply presented as a love interest with affected literary tastes. Later in the play, she demonstrates her own agency, wit and courage by charming her way through the Spanish lines to bring food to the starving French troops at the Siege of Arras. This grand Romantic gesture springs from her own deep feelings of love aroused by the soldier who has been writing love letters to her – she believes him to be Christian, but, of course, he is Cyrano. When Christian dies in battle at the Siege of Arras, Cyrano, despite knowing that he has won Roxane's love, makes a further grand gesture of self-denial by protecting her from the painful truth of their deception. This denial lasts for years, until the moments before his own death, when he can at last reveal to his beloved that he is, in fact, the man whose words won her heart, so many years before.

The play, then, is full of grand, emotionally driven and impulsive gestures that spring from deep and, we presume, despite all the artifice in the drama, authentic feelings. The poignancy of the performances is intensified by the fact that the lovers are all doomed – none of the loving relationships established in the play is consummated. At the very moment Christian and Roxane are married, Christian is dragged off to war; and at the very moment when Cyrano reveals his love for Roxane and she returns it, he dies. On one level, we appreciate that the events unfolding on stage are absurd (why doesn't he just *tell* her earlier?); but, on another, we are moved by the depth of passion that motivates the near-farcical outcomes. This series of emotionally powerful absurdities is what a heroic tragi-comedy is all about.

Activities

What do you understand by Classicism and the Romantic movement? Look up the terms in an encyclopaedia, either in print or online. How do the entries describe Classicism and Romanticism in art, drama and literature? If you reflect on your own life, do you yourself uphold the values of Classicism or Romanticism – or are you a mixture of both? That is, as values, do you prefer harmony to discord, formal balance to spontaneous irregularity, restraint to exaggeration, artifice to authenticity, society to the individual, culture to nature, or, *vice versa*? Are the characters in *Cyrano* purely Classicists, purely Romanticists, or are they a mixture of both?

How helpful is it to know something about the dramatists, poets, philosophers, scientists and artists mentioned in the play, if only in passing (e.g. Balthazar Baro, Jean Chapelain, Nicolas Copernicus, Philippe de Champaigne)? What pleasures are there for an audience, more generally, in recognising in a play or film characters from an 'extended universe'? In groups, choose some of the names mentioned in the play (many are identified more fully in the Glossary to this Scotnote) and track them down on the internet. Find out something about their lives and work, in the original French or in translation. Does this knowledge add to the richness of your appreciation of the play? If you were writing a play that is situated at the heart of the cultural world of the twenty-first century, right now, which 'iconic' figures from the world of drama, film, television, art and literature would you choose to have cameos, to prop up the bar, or simply to mention? And how would you explain their cultural significance to an audience five hundred years from now?

4. CHARACTERS IN THE PLAY

The main characters in the play are, as we have seen, Cyrano, Christian, Roxane and De Guiche. Cyrano and Christian are Cadets, that is, minor noblemen who are serving as soldiers. Most of the regiment are outsiders, Gascons from the French countryside, stationed in the urban centre of Paris. Cyrano is the archetypal, eloquent Romantic outsider and individualist: he refuses to accept patronage as it will curb his freedom of speech, he calls out hypocrisy where he finds it, and he is unafraid to do battle with his enemies in defence of his principles. Christian is a new recruit to the Cadets, brave enough to insult Cyrano by making mocking reference to his nose when warned not to do so, but he is tongue-tied in the presence of a beautiful woman. De Guiche is a senior military officer who is put in charge of the Cadets. As we have seen, Roxane can be described as a *précieuse*, that is, one of a recognisable group of female intellectuals, prominent in seventeenth-century Paris, who attended salons and enjoyed lively conversation, wit and wordplay.

The fact that there are four roles complicates the stereotypical dynamics of the love triangle: there is a female object of affection (Roxane), *two* male lovers (Cyrano/Christian), and a rival (De Guiche). The collaboration of Cyrano and Christian in the role of male lover raises a number of questions. What is their relationship to each other? Are they partners or rivals? Which will Roxane ultimately choose? Will De Guiche unmask their deception?

Cyrano and Christian can, at the outset, assume a single role because their characters are complementary: Cyrano is ugly but witty while Christian is handsome but inarticulate. Together, they represent the ideal partner for Roxane, who, at the start of the play, demands both beauty and wit from her lover. The character of De Guiche, an older, married man who desires Roxane, and takes spiteful revenge when he realises he cannot have her, is a comic butt for the wit of Roxane and Cyrano, and a dramatic means of intensifying the threat to the happiness of the younger lovers.

All the characters develop, at least to some extent, as the play progresses. Roxane, principally, through Cyrano's letters to her, comes to realise that the inner soul is more beautiful than outward appearance, and eventually chooses the 'Cyrano' half of her ideal lover. Christian, initially content to allow Cyrano to provide the expressions of love that he himself cannot formulate, eventually realises that he has lost Roxane's love, and nobly dies in battle. Cyrano, whose shame about his own appearance makes him believe he can never be worthy of Roxane's love, comes to understand that Roxane does indeed love him – but his loyalty to Christian forbids him from revealing their joint deception to Roxane until the point of his death. De Guiche perhaps undergoes the most remarkable transformation of all. While he begins the play almost as a pantomime villain, plotting for Roxane to be married to one of his lackeys so that he may seduce her himself, then sending Christian off to war in the immediate aftermath of his marriage to Roxane, and, finally, condemning Christian and Cyrano's troop of Cadets to a suicide mission at the Siege of Arras, he redeems himself by arranging for Roxane's escape from the siege, and ends the play as Roxane's honourable friend and confidant. He expresses his admiration for the constancy of Cyrano's principles, and laments his own compromises in his rise to power and status. And he attempts, unsuccessfully, to warn Cyrano of the murder plot that will ultimately take his life.

Throughout the play, De Guiche functions as a contrast to Cyrano: he is unprincipled whereas Cyrano cleaves to his personal code of honour; he makes compromises whereas

Cyrano remains his own man; and he is therefore successful in his career whereas Cyrano ends up being marginalised and impoverished. What is perhaps surprising is that by the end of the play De Guiche acknowledges his own failings and becomes effectively Cyrano's ally.

If De Guiche's character inspires contempt and sympathy at different times in the play, then perhaps so does Cyrano's. Despite his own, and others', repeated profession of his honour, principles and integrity, he does, after all, attempt to win Roxane's love by an act of deception. We might argue in his defence that he resorts to ventriloquism, with Christian as his dummy, because he is convinced that his physical appearance will repel her, and so his deception is the inevitable, tragic outcome of a profound passion for Roxane and an equally profound self-loathing. When Christian dies, we might understand Cyrano's refusal to reveal himself to Roxane as an acknowledgement that he has betrayed his own principles, and his self-denial is a form of atonement.

We might also argue that our engagement with the main characters in the basic love triangle of Roxane, Cyrano and Christian is, in part, a result of our sympathetic frustration with all of them. We want Roxane to recognise Cyrano's love for her in the early scenes of the play, and we are frustrated when she is beguiled by Christian's beauty. We admire Christian's courage in baiting Cyrano in their first encounter, and we are frustrated when he cannot match his bravery with wit. We want Cyrano to abandon his self-loathing and we feel frustrated when he fails to realise that his passion, charisma and wit are sufficient to win Roxane's heart. But the love triangle also leaves the audience with a dilemma: even if the three characters manage to overcome their flaws and their misperceptions, Roxane would still have to make a choice between two worthy suitors. Someone has to lose. Which of the characters, in which we are invited to invest our sympathy, will end up being disappointed? There is, as Morgan hints in his introduction to his translation, the possibility of reading a gay subtext into *Cyrano*, a possibility justified by the apparent homosexuality of the real-life Cyrano. Morgan suggests that such a subtext may be 'scarcely but perhaps just audible in the play itself' (p. x). It has to be said that evidence for such a reading of either the original play or its translation is indeed 'scarcely audible'. It is manifestly clear that both Cyrano and Christian are in love with Roxane, and she reciprocates this love. What complicates matters is that, for her, Cyrano and Christian are one person, an idealised lover who combines Christian's physical attraction with Cyrano's soul and wit. In order to win Roxane's love, Cyrano and Christian must therefore unite their complementary qualities, physical and spiritual, and, insofar as romantic desire might be understood as an aspiration towards a spiritual union with the other, it might be argued that the two male suitors become united in their mutual aspiration to win Roxane. However, there is no evidence in the text of the play that Cyrano and Christian feel any physical attraction towards each other. As David Kinloch (2004) observes, there are motifs in Cyrano's situation that are familiar to gay lovers and which resonate with traditional interpretations of homosexual love: given society's censure, gay lovers must often suppress the explicit avowal of their love, and resort to disguised encounters, in darkness. There is also, in the relationship between Christian and Cyrano, a desire for completion in that each can provide what the other cannot. In certain respects, then, there are elements of *Cyrano* that can speak to gay experience, even though, as Kinloch (2004: 141) acknowledges: 'Cyrano is not gay. He is in love with Roxane, not Christian.'

Activity

Choose some of the main and minor characters in *Cyrano* (e.g. Cyrano, Christian, Roxane, De Guiche, Valvert, Ragueneau, Le Bret/Carbon, Montfleury) and note down some of the qualities, positive and negative, that they represent (e.g. sincerity, honour, courage, beauty, deformity, hypocrisy, manipulation, (dis)loyalty, generosity, spite, nature, artifice, and so on). Can you then situate the characters in relations of contrast, similarity and complementarity? In what ways do Cyrano's qualities complement Christian's? In what ways do they both complement Roxane? How do they contrast with De Guiche and Valvert? How does Cyrano contrast with Montfleury? In what ways is he similar to Ragueneau? Can you map out changing relations of similarity, contrast and complementarity as the play develops?

5. FOOTING

One systematic way of thinking about the issues of performance, character and ethics that we have raised above is to consider what the American sociologist, Erving Goffman called 'footing'. Goffman was interested in the ways in which everyday talk and conversational interactions actively construct the self, both publicly and privately. One of the features of interaction that is crucially important in the construction of the self is, according to Goffman, 'footing.' 'Footing' can be generally defined as the role or roles the speaker adopts in any interaction. There are a number of factors that need to be taken into consideration when we consider what the footing is in any given conversational exchange. Scholars after Goffman (e.g. Levinson, 1988) have debated these factors and given them different names, but for the purposes of this Scotnote, we can think of a conversational interaction as being made up of the following elements:

- The *source* or author of the words uttered
- The *speaker* of the words uttered
- The *addressee* to whom the words uttered are directed
- The acknowledged *audience* of the words uttered
- The unacknowledged *eavesdroppers* who overhear the words uttered.

If we consider the footings, or participant roles in this way, we can see quite clearly how performance and character are constructed using different footings in different episodes in the play. In Act 1, Scene 4; pp. 23–25, for example, there is a flyting (a ritual exchange of insults) and then a duel between Cyrano and Valvert, in which Cyrano imagines the insults Valvert might have directed towards him, and then fences with him, while composing an impromptu poem. The footing in this scene is quite complicated. During the flyting scene Cyrano is the source and the speaker of his words. However, he invites us to imagine that Valvert is the source and the speaker, and that he himself is the addressee. All this is done, however, in the knowledge that an audience is watching and the Cyrano-Valvert interaction is performed primarily to show off to that audience. As the flyting becomes a duel, Cyrano remains the source and speaker of the words, Valvert becomes the addressee, but the audience is still the main reason for the exchange taking place at all. The interaction between a speaker and an addressee for the sake of an audience is, of course, a hallmark of theatrical performance, and the exchange represents Cyrano's performance of a public self. To add to the complexity of this scene, the *real* audience in the actual theatre (or the reader of the text) is put in the position of an eavesdropper, an unacknowledged listener or group of listeners that overhears what the acknowledged on-stage audience is attending to.

The participant roles are differently distributed in the balcony episode in Act 3, Scenes 6–9, where Christian woos Roxane, prompted by Cyrano. In the early scenes, Cyrano is the source of the words, Christian is the speaker who utters them, and Roxane is the addressee and the audience, someone who also believes that source and speaker are the same. The actual audience in the theatre again takes on the role of eavesdropper. As the scenes continue, Cyrano takes over the role of speaker from Christian, and so the roles of source and speaker are indeed fused, as Roxane believes them to be. However, she misattributes the identity of the speaker, believing him to be Christian.

As the play comes to a close, in Act 5, Scene 5, Cyrano, now fatally wounded, reads what Roxane believes is Christian's final, bloodstained letter aloud to her. As he begins, Cyrano is both the source and the speaker, although Roxane, who is again both addressee and audience, still mistakenly believes the source of the words to be Christian. By the end of the exchange, however, Roxane understands that Cyrano is both the speaker *and* the source of the words. The eavesdropping audience at last sees something that is unusual in the development of this particular love triangle: a speaker, in the role of his private self, performs his own words to an individual addressee who is also the primary audience, and they finally acknowledge each other's true identity.

These three key episodes are analysed further in later sections of this Scotnote. For the time being, it is sufficient to note that there is quite a different distribution of participant roles, or footings, in each of these episodes. In the first, Cyrano is speaker and source, but the addressee (Valvert) and acknowledged audience are distinct. In the second, the addressee and acknowledged audience are one person (i.e. Roxane) and Cyrano is at first the source but not the speaker. When he assumes both roles, he is misidentified by the addressee. In the third, he is both speaker and source, but the addressee/acknowledged audience (Roxane again) only gradually comes to realise this fact. The different distributions of the participant roles distinguish the footings that give each episode in the play a distinct character. In the first we see the public Cyrano, playing to an audience; in the second, we see the private Cyrano, whose audience is the woman he can only address via, or in the guise of, another; and in the final scene we see the private Cyrano at last addressing his beloved, honestly and openly.

Activity

Take any extended scene or collection of scenes from the play and analyse its footing. That is, identify the *source* or author of the words uttered, the *speaker* of the words uttered, the *addressee* to whom the words uttered are directed, the *acknowledged audience* of the words uttered, and the *unacknowledged eavesdroppers* who overhear the words uttered. The last of these is probably going to be you! Pay particular attention to those scenes in which the source and the speaker are not the same, and those in which the addressee and the on-stage audience are not the same. How do changes in footing change the way we think about the characters – e.g. about their sincerity, and their performance of public/private selves?

6. *CYRANO* IN SCOTS

Of course, one of the characteristics that distinguishes Morgan's version of *Cyrano* from other translations and versions is that it is in Scots. In his introduction to the published version of the play, Morgan (1992, p. xi) writes:

> Various English versions of the play have been made, but it is one of those rich and challenging works which need to be translated again and again, in different circumstances and for different purposes, readerly and actorly. The time seemed ripe for a Scottish version, but one that would be thoroughly stageworthy, and not incomprehensible to audiences at the Edinburgh International Festival. I decided that an urban Glaswegian Scots would offer the best basis, since it is widely spoken, can accommodate contemporary reference, and is no means incapable of the lyrical and the poetic, and comes unburdened by the baggage of the older Scots which used to be thought suitable for historical plays. I kept English for the Count De Guiche, and for some of the minor characters (the fops, nuns, Roxane's duenna).

This brief comment raises a number of interesting points which can be taken up and developed further. First, Morgan notes that the 'time seemed ripe' for a Scottish version. We might ask why. David Kinloch in his discussion of the play (Kinloch, 2004) begins by noting that the first performances of this Scots version of Rostand's patriotic 'heroic comedy' coincided with a particularly dark time in Scotland's aspirations to self-government, and it might be regarded, as many cultural productions of that period are, as an assertion of Scottish national identity in the face of political disappointment. Elsewhere (Corbett, 2012), I have argued that Communicado commissioned Morgan to script his version of *Cyrano* at a time when Rostand's play was enjoying considerable public prominence in the francophone and anglophone world, with various theatrical and cinematic versions and adaptations circulating. Moreover, Morgan would have been very conscious of half a century of critically and commercially successful Scots translations and adaptations of French and Italian comedies, often for the Edinburgh International Festival. These were frequently translations of Molière, beginning with Robert Kemp's *L'École des femmes/Let Wives tak Tent* in 1948, and continuing with Liz Lochhead's version of *Tartuffe*, which was premiered to acclaim in 1985 and revived in 1987. While Kemp's translation, like a number of historical plays, draws on the 'older Scots' that Morgan refers to in his introduction, his friend, Liz Lochhead's version was much more contemporary and urban in its use of Scots.

Morgan no doubt wished to emulate Lochhead's success, and, like her, decided that, for his translation, an urban Glasgwegian Scots would offer the best basis for his translated text. It is important to pay attention to his precise wording here: Morgan is *not* claiming that his translation is a naturalistic or accurate representation of spoken language in Glasgow. Rather, urban Glasgow speech provides a *basis* for an extended, literary idiom that can incorporate references from contemporary popular culture and extend to lyrical and poetic passages.

Thus it is that Morgan's *Cyrano* represents a complex layering of different kinds of language. While Morgan claims his Scots is based on urban Glasgow speech, few of the expressions are wholly confined to the city and its inhabitants. Some are slang expressions that have a storied history, like 'get a jildy oan' (*hurry up*), an expression originally deriving from the Hindi 'juldee', which is also found in Liz Lochhead's plays.

The expression 'jildy jildy' or 'juldee juldee' is shared with English slang, and derives from the years of British colonial expansion in India. There is dictionary evidence associating 'bampot' (*idiot*) with the urban centres of Glasgow and Dundee, but the word is also shared with English slang.

There are also plenty of more widely-used Scots expressions, like 'wheen' (*somewhat, a bit*), 'wabbit' (*exhausted*), 'clairty' (*filthy*), and 'syne' (*rinse* or *wash*). In the flyting with Valvert, Morgan's Cyrano describes his nose as a 'lang whang', literally a long strip of leather or ribbon, but here no doubt referring to the Lang Whang, a common name for the old Edinburgh–Lanark road, in particular, as the *Dictionary of the Scots Language* reminds us, 'the stretch between Balerno and Carnwath where it passes over open moorland'. Most of these expressions and references are contemporary: the *Dictionary of the Scots Language* has a good number of twentieth-century citations, from Glasgow and also other parts of the country.

The written text of the play indicates that much of its 'Scottishness' comes from accent as much as vocabulary. The 'phonetic spellings' of words that are common to both Scots and English suggest that the actors should pronounce the words with a Glasgow accent. 'Phonetic spellings' are, here, adaptations of standard orthography usually to indicate localised pronunciations, though some like 'uz' (*us*) are used primarily to make the text *look* Scots. They are evident in passages such as the following (Act 3, Scene 7; p. 93), when Cyrano, hidden in the shadows, addresses Roxane:

> Wae ivry look ye gie me Ah kin win
> Tae something new and clean and keen! Ye kin
> Begin tae unnerston, weigh, suss, it, me?
> Tae sense the daurk, and ma soul, risin free ...?

There are no distinctly Scots vocabulary items in these four lines, and their Scots flavour is largely thanks to the spellings: 'wae' (*with*), 'ivry' (*every*) 'gie' (*give*), 'Ah' (*I*), 'kin' (*can*), tae (*to*), 'unnerston' (*understand*), 'daurk' (*dark*), 'ma' (*my*), 'risin' (*rising*). Like many writers in Scots, Morgan does not worry too much about the consistency of his spellings and so we find a number of variants of the same word when we read the text. For example, at different points in the text, the positive and negative forms of the verb *have* are expressed in traditional Scots spellings as well as more innovative phonetic variations: 'hae', 'hasnae', 'hiz', 'hisnae', 'hivnae', 'havin'.

The basis of Glaswegian Scots, then, is grounded on a few relatively localised urban Scots expressions (e.g 'mollocate', *beat up* or *batter*) supplemented by a larger number of Scots expressions and references (e.g. to the Lang Whang, and to the Glasgow-born newspaper caricaturist, Emilio Coia) that have contemporary currency both in and beyond Glasgow. Additionally, many words that are shared with English are written in their Scottish forms ('give/gie') or given 'phonetic' spellings ('every/ivry').

As they may not be in every Glasgow speaker's – or every Scots speaker's – active vocabulary nowadays, distinctively Scots vocabulary items are actually used relatively sparsely in the dialogue in the translation. As Morgan insists, the play has to be 'stageworthy', and that means being intelligible to an audience. The 'Scottishness' of the play comes in part from the insistence on a Scottish accent for the majority of the characters – the villain, De Guiche, being one of the few marked out as using English.

At certain points in the play, there are explicit references to the fact that the homeland of the Gascon cadets is not Paris but rural Gascony. That is, the urban Scots idiom of the translation is not in fact their mother tongue. To convey this,

Morgan switches occasionally into rural North-East Scots, drawing also on the older Scots expressions that he avoids elsewhere in the play, as in Act 4, Scene 10; p. 143:

> CYRANO (*speaks some Gascon*)
> *Braw loons, divnae draa baack!*
>   We're no deid yet!
> Two deaths tae avenge: Christian's and ma set
> A happy hopes! – That flag! Her lace, her monogram!
> *Fa's radgie ti camshaschle them!*
>   (*to the fifer:*) Pley! No a psalm!

Here Cyrano's exhortations to his fellow Cadets (which might be glossed as '*Brave lads, don't withdraw! ... Who's crazy enough to put them in chains?*') employ forms that suggest North East Scots: the negative auxiliary verb 'divnae' ('don't'), the elongated vowel in 'baack' and the initial consonant in 'fa' ('who'). It is significant, however, that in his internal monologue ('Two deaths tae avenge ...'), he switches back to the 'Glaswegian' variety that is thus presented as the 'natural' idiom of the play.

The next sections of this Scotnote turn to three key episodes in the play which are discussed in close detail. To some degree, the themes and issues discussed above are illustrated and expanded upon in the following discussion. Page references are again to the Carcanet edition (Morgan, 1992).

Activity

Take a scene from the play and list all the expressions that you consider to be 'Scots'. Review your list and subdivide the expressions into (a) words and phrases that are common between Scots and English but are given Scottish forms, e.g. 'ivry' (every), 'unnerston' (understand) or 'gie' (give), and (b) those vocabulary items that seem to be distinctively Scots, e.g. 'keek' (look) or 'wheen' (a little). Look up the items in Group (b) in the online *Dictionary of the Scots Language* at **www.dsl.ac.uk**. When you find the items, look at the citations. Are the expressions still current? Are there citations from different geographical regions?

Using the information you have gathered, think critically about Morgan's claim that the play employs contemporary 'urban Glaswegian Scots' as a 'basis'. What does this actually mean?

7. THREE KEY EPISODES

i. The Flyting and Duel with Valvert (Act 1, Scene 4, pp. 15–30)

The early scenes in the play introduce Cyrano to the audience via a series of confrontations which afford him the opportunity to demonstrate his principles, wit and courage. An enjoyable characteristic of Act 1, Scene 4 is the extravagance of the insults that Cyrano devises to taunt his enemies – while based on Rostand's original text, this aspect of the scene also recalls the long Scottish tradition of 'flytings,' or poems of ritual insult, practised by such poets as William Dunbar and Walter Kennedy, Robert Burns, and, latterly, Robert Crawford and W. N. Herbert. Cyrano appears dramatically as a 'voice' towards the end of Act 1, Scene 3; p. 15, addressing the actor, Montfleury, with the line 'Eejit, Ah gave ye wan month aff the boards!', that is 'Idiot, I warned you to keep away from the stage for a month!' Scene 4 begins with the confrontation between Montfleury, who, with the encouragement of the audience, attempts to continue playing his role in Baro's Classical drama, *Clorise*, and Cyrano, who threatens him with violence unless he exits immediately. While there are several motives for Cyrano's anger, one is explicitly aesthetic (p. 16):

CYRANO
                              No away yet?
        Right, Ah'll take the stage and dish him, get
        That thick Bologna sausage in the slicerama!
MONTFLEURY
        Sir, if you insult me, you insult Drama!
CYRANO
        You and the Muse are total strangers, but
        If you did happen to meet, she'd stoap yer strut.

> She'd scunner, fatso, at her wobbling fruit,
> And kick yer backside wi her classic boot.

In these lines we see Cyrano position himself against the current fashion in drama, which Montfleury claims to represent. At this point, the on-stage audience, and particularly the nobility and bourgeoisie, side with Montfleury and condemn Cyrano, who insults and threatens them all. When challenged by a young man to explain why he hates Montfleury so, after the actor eventually does depart, Cyrano replies (p. 19):

> The double answer,
> My dear young silly fella, is argument-proof.
> *First,* he's a hopeless ham, raises the roof
> And humphs his verses with a porter's sweat
> When they should glide and soar! – *Second,* let
> That be ma secret ...

Cyrano's aesthetic principles are now coupled with a secret reason for hating Montfleury, which, we later learn, is that the actor has attempted to flirt with Roxane. Meanwhile he berates the author of the play, Balthazar Baro, as an 'Old blunderbuss,/Baro's verse is rated worse than zero,/It's made for interruption!' (pp. 19–20), an opinion that causes the Lady Intellectuals in the audience practically to faint.

As we observed earlier, then, Cyrano is initially established as a new kind of dramatic hero, in opposition to Classical actors such as Montfleury, and Classical plays such as those written by Baro. His antipathy to Montfleury is not purely based on critical taste, however; his actions are also bound up in his own concealed passion for Roxane and his desire to defend her against Montfleury's carnal desire. Ironically, he will soon become a willing vehicle to promote another suitor's desire to possess the woman he himself secretly loves. The members of the audience who have paid to see Montfleury perform are, not unnaturally, aggrieved and angry with Cyrano, even after he throws money into the crowd to compensate them for the abandonment of the play. The angry exchanges quickly turn to the subject of Cyrano's outsize nose, and he dares a reluctant Troublemaker to insult his appearance. At the prompting of the villain, De Guiche, his lackey, Valvert, attempts to silence Cyrano by lamely observing that his nose is 'gey big, it's clear'. In response, Cyrano launches into an extravagant and witty series of potential insults that Valvert could have directed at his appearance, in a breath-taking range of styles, from 'thuggish' to 'practical' via 'gracious', 'pedantic', 'lyrical', and others. Cyrano ends by warning Valvert that while he can mock his own appearance, he will hurt others who attempt to do the same. Valvert is incensed that he is being ridiculed by a soldier of lower social status than himself, and the upshot of their continued quarrel is that they take up their swords and fight a duel, during which Cyrano improvises an appropriate *ballade*: three verses of eight lines each, followed by one four-line verse. This poetic duel becomes, for the on-stage audience, an acceptable substitute for the Classical drama that they have been denied. It also represents Cyrano's preferred dramatic form: a display of (apparently spontaneous) wit, and a performance stemming from genuine emotion. During the performance, Cyrano again identifies himself as a representative of authentic poetry (p. 28):

> I slowly undo and discard
> My cloak that's so funky and furrish,
> Unscabbard my glittering sword
> With the elegance of a bard [...]

On the final line of the *ballade*, Cyrano, as promised, strikes Valvert and wounds him, winning the duel. The crowd's enthusiastic response endorses the duel as new kind of performance art, one fop crying out, 'Avant-garde!' (p. 29). Even D'Artagnan, the hero of Alexandre Dumas' *The Three Musketeers*, praises Cyrano and shakes his hand, and, as the crowd disperses, Cyrano admits to his friend, Le Bret/Carbon, that he has used all his monthly salary in throwing money to the crowd as compensation. When chided as 'daft', Cyrano says 'Whit a gesture though!' (p. 30).

This scene, then, introduces Cyrano as a Romantic hero who cannot resist making a grand gesture. This is the public Cyrano: principled in his aesthetic taste, ingenious in his own artistry, unafraid to confront a crowd or duel with a social superior. There are also hints of the private Cyrano, the man acutely sensitive to what he regards as his own physical deformity, and harbouring a secret motive for detesting Montfleury that goes beyond the actor's incompetence and poor choice of roles.

Act 1 Scene 4 also showcases the brilliance of Morgan's verse, which has to rise to the challenge of showing that Cyrano's 'spontaneous' discourse outshines Montfleury's scripted, Classical bombast. In the previous scene, we have been subjected to only a little of Montfleury performing Baro's play, in stilted English (p. 14):

> Happy is he who leaves the courts behind,
> In solitude communing with the wind,
> And who, when Zephyr breathes about the woods ...

In the following scene, this outdated verse is contrasted with Cyrano's extravagant flyting, by which he demonstrates to Valvert what he might have said to insult him (p. 25):

> MILITARY: 'Pynt yer supergun at the troops!'
> PRACTICAL: 'Ye kin raffle it, cowp the coops,
> Hit the jackpot, snaffle the dosh and away!'

Or lastly, parodying Pyramus in the play:
'See how this nose has blasted the harmony
Of its master's features! It blushes wretchedly!'
That's a wee tait a what ye could've sayed
If ye'd had wit or kulchur [...]

Cyrano amply demonstrates his command of poetic verse, moving easily from clever rhymes in Scots to an elegant English parody of a couplet from a play, *Pyramus and Thisbe* (1623) by another French playwright who was popular at the Hôtel de Bourgogne, Théophile de Viau (or Viaud). The story of Pyramus and Thisbe is better known to anglophone audiences from its parodic performance by the rustics in Shakespeare's *A Midsummer Night's Dream* (1595/6). Viau's original lines in his version of the story are *'Ah voici le poignard qui du sang de son maître/S'est souillé lâchement. Il en rougit, le traître!*' (literally,' Ah here is the dagger that with his master's blood/Is stained cowardly. It blushes, the traitor!' Cyrano substitutes his nose for Viau's dagger). Thus, Cyrano is demonstrating that his 'wit' and 'culture' are superior both to those of Valvert and to the dramatic tradition represented by Montfleury and Baro. As readers, or as members of the actual theatre audience, we are invited to align ourselves with the on-stage audience which is seduced by Cyrano's public performance into abandoning Classical aesthetics and attitudes in favour of grand Romantic gestures. One of the functions of Act 1, Scene 4, in fact, is to teach us – or remind us – how to respond to and appreciate the kind of play that *Cyrano* epitomises.

Activity

Act 1, Scenes 3 and 4 offer the actors a rich variety of performing styles and traditions. In Scene 3, how would you stage and perform Montfleury's brief declamation of the lines, in English, from Baro's play? How would you demonstrate a contrast with the dynamism of Cyrano's interruption in Scots? In Scene 4, during the flyting with Valvert, how would you show through your own acting, or through your directions to an actor, the versatility of Cyrano's own performance, which moves quickly from 'Thuggish' to 'Freen-like', 'Descriptive', 'Pawky', 'Gracious', and 'Truculent', all the way to 'Practical' (pp. 24–25)? How would you change your pace, intonation and gestures to convey 'a plan/For each, tae suit yer tone o voice'? What advice would you give to the actor playing Valvert, to help him demonstrate his incompetence?

ii. The Wooing of Roxane (Act 3, Scene 7, pp 88–94)

The balcony scene, in which Christian and Cyrano collaborate in the wooing of Roxane, reveals the private face of Cyrano, but only insofar as it is masked by Christian's outward appearance. At the start of the scene, when Roxane is alerted by chuckies, or small pebbles, thrown against her window, she asks 'Who's that?' which receives the response from Christian 'It's me.' She asks again, 'Who's 'me'?' and the reply is simply, 'Christian.' This is, of course, not entirely true.

Roxane is a young and inexperienced lover; she still idealises romantic love, influenced by the plays, lectures and performances she is shown as attending so frequently. She is not yet able to distinguish between physical and spiritual love, and so she cannot yet tell their representatives, Christian and Cyrano, apart. She is attracted by Christian's physical good looks, but she demands the articulation of a spiritual devotion that he cannot give. This needs to be articulated by Cyrano. The two suitors combine into an ideal but impossible lover. At the start of the balcony scene she has been disappointed in Christian's earlier, tongue-tied failure to declare his love to her in the style that she demands, and so, now, Christian,

Edwin Morgan's *Cyrano de Bergerac*

prompted by Cyrano, has to win her back. He begins to do so by adopting poetic language to describe his passion: he develops an extended metaphor in which his infant love, personified, is cradled in a cruel net of nerves, and his soul is the 'bassinet', or crib. When Roxane asks why he did not simply 'snuff oot' his new-born passion, he reaches for a Classical allusion: his love is like the infant, Hercules, who, according to Greek mythology, strangled two snakes that attacked him in his cradle (pp. 88–89):

ROXANE
        Good! But if it was cruel, why'd ye not
        Snuff oot that chancy love, there in its cot?
CHRISTIAN
        Ah tried, Madame, but Ah ... hud tae cry keys
        This ... puny squaller ... wis a Hercules ...
ROXANE
        Keep it up.
CHRISTIAN
        ... that strangled ... the two snakes
        Of Pride and Doot ... like that!

In adapting the legend of the infant Hercules to his own purposes, Cyrano/Christian mixes familiar playground language (*tae cry keys* 'to call a truce, as in a playground game') and Classical references. This unexpected mixing of the vernacular and familiar with high Classical subject matter is characteristic both of Cyrano's poetic style and Morgan's translation strategy.

As can be seen in the exchange quoted above, Christian is hesitant in his responses to Roxane, and so Cyrano, the source of the words, soon takes over the speaking role too. This shift in participant roles changes the 'footing' of the scene. At last Cyrano can talk for himself about his private passion, and he can do so directly to the object of his adoration, but only because she thinks she is listening to Christian. As soon as he begins to speak for himself, he and Roxane fall into an easy, imaginative and affectionate banter. Cyrano acknowledges that the darkness gives him the unfamiliar security and courage to express his private self honestly (pp. 90–91):

ROXANE
    It's true, yer voice soonds different, more and more.

CYRANO
    Aye, it's quite different. The night's ma gaird and grot.
    Here Ah kin daur tae be me, kin daur ...
                               But what –
    Ah don't know – aw this – forgie me – stealin
    Ower me, new and wunnerfu, the feelin ...

ROXANE
    It's new?

CYRANO
    It's new ... totally ... tae be sincere ...
    My hert ay nippit ... tae be laughed at ... the fear ...

In his annotations in the margins of his own copy of the published version of the play, Morgan glossed 'nippit' as 'constricted, inhibited'. The moment is revealing of Cyrano's character: the brave cadet who enthusiastically faces and defeats a hundred assailants in defence of a friend is afraid of being laughed at by his beloved, his heart is inhibited, and so he has difficulty in being 'sincere'. The irony is that only by engaging in deception alongside Christian can his sincerity be expressed.

Edwin Morgan's *Cyrano de Bergerac*

The scene also allows Morgan to demonstrate that a vernacular idiom based on Glasgow speech can rise to the lyrical intensity necessary to win Roxane's heart, which it does (p. 93):

CYRANO
    Ma wurds and ma praise
    Huv made her trimmle between the blue sprays.
    Aye, ye're trimmlin like a leaf amang the leaves!
    Ye're trimmlin, Ah kin feel it, your hon, yer sleeves
    Unknowinly thrill oot a trimmlin doon
    Alang the jasmine branches where Ah swoon!
ROXANE
    Ah'm trimmlin, aye, and greetin, Ah love ye,
    Ah'm yours!
    Ye've gote me drunk wae it!

At this point, the moment of Cyrano's conquest of Roxane's heart, Christian interrupts with a demand for a kiss. The switch from a profession of spiritual adoration to a demand for physical expression of love is comic, and Cyrano is startled. Roxane, however, is eager to oblige. Again, we see that she has not yet learned to distinguish spiritual devotion from physical attraction. Before the issue is resolved, a Capuchin monk enters with a message for Roxane.

Activity

There is a progression in this scene from hesitancy to confidence, first as Christian stammers his words, prompted by Cyrano, and then Cyrano takes over, finding in himself, as he speaks, a new-found freedom to express his true feelings. Read the scene again and try to plot the moments when the emotional changes occur. How would you advise the actors to perform their lines to show this increasing confidence? Pay particular attention, too, to the character of Roxane. Is she just a passive recipient of the lines performed by her suitors? Is she simply a victim of their deceit? How do her demands and her responses motivate the actions of her suitors? To what extent does she also have independent agency in the scene? Is she a sympathetic character to the audience at this point?

iii. The Death of Cyrano
(Act 5, Scenes 5 & 6, pp. 152–63)

The final two scenes of the play take place fifteen years after the action shown in the first four Acts, that is, the wooing of Roxane and the Siege of Arras. During that siege, Roxane had declared her love for Christian's 'soul', unaware that in doing so she was in fact indicating her love for Cyrano. Christian then died in battle, and Cyrano, to honour his memory, allowed Roxane to continue to believe that Christian was the author of the letters that so inspired her love. For fifteen years, Roxane has lived the life of a widow in a convent, attended to by nuns. During this time, Cyrano visits her every week to entertain her with news and gossip, in what he calls his 'gazette'.

As Act 5, Scene 5 opens the audience knows, but Roxane does not, that Cyrano has been fatally wounded by an assassin. He makes his excuse that he has been delayed by 'a visit Ah could well dae without', that is, by a 'nuisancess' that, implicitly, is Death. He teases Sister Marthe, one of the nuns, who observes his frailty, and he faints when trying to deliver his news. On his recovery, he asks to read the bloodstained letter that Roxane keeps close to her heart, and she agrees. As he reads the letter aloud, Roxane begins to understand that he is both the speaker and the author of the words, and she recognises the voice that won her heart in the earlier balcony scene. Cyrano, however, denies his authorship of the letter.

The exchanges between Roxane and Cyrano again revolve around the themes of performance and sincerity. 'Ye read it so well, that letter!' Roxane exclaims (p. 156) before realising that Cyrano is not simply performing the words of another. When she realises that it has become too dark for Cyrano to see the text on the page, she remonstrates with him (p. 157):

– And fur thae fourteen years he pleyed the role
Of an auld freen, sae light-hertit and droll ...

And she exclaims 'That sowl wis yours!' (p. 158) when she recalls the night on the balcony. Cyrano continues to deny this, but in doing so contradicts himself: 'Naw, naw, dear love. Ah didnae love ye, naw' (p. 158). When Roxane demands to know why Cyrano has continued the deception, he responds that while the tears on the letter were not Christian's, 'the bluid is his' (p. 158). Again, the spirituality of Cyrano is inseparable from the physicality of Christian. They cannot be considered a single, individual lover. This fact is acknowledged and lamented by Roxane in the later line 'Jist wan Ah loved, and twice he's gone fae me!' (p. 161).

It is left to Cyrano to die in suitable style. He complains that he had wished to have 'a swordsman's death' (p. 159) rather than being the victim of an ambush. In an apparent digression, the poetry-loving pastry-cook, Ragueneau, enters the scene to inform Cyrano that he is now working with the playwright, Molière, a representative of the new style of drama, who is becoming famous partly because he steals, or plagiarises, Cyrano's work. The relevance of this digression becomes clearer when Cyrano announces that he now accepts his role as the author of words that others receive credit for (p. 160):

> It's fair; wae wan fit in the grave, ma mood
> Says Molière's a genius, Christian looked good!

With these lines, Cyrano announces that he is content with having been the source of sentiments that others utter in public. Thus reconciled, he prepares to meet Death for the last time, and to go with her to spend his afterlife on the moon, alongside his fellow philosophers and scientists, Socrates and Galileo. He struggles to his feet, and imagines that he is fighting his old enemies, Lies and Compromise, on his way to the gates of heaven. Then, as he enters, he bows low and flourishes his 'plume', the large feather on his hat.

Morgan translates as 'Ma plume' the final words of Rostand's original play, which are '*Mon panache*'. The word 'panache', which in French indeed refers to the flamboyant tuft of feathers that adorned gentlemen's hats in the seventeenth century, entered anglophone culture in the late nineteenth century with the transferred meaning of 'display' or 'swagger,' largely as a result of English translations of Rostand's play. Cyrano's final words and his dying gesture, then, need to convey the *panache* of the original text, and the reader or audience might be aware of this if they are acquainted with the original French text, or its various English translations. The nature of Cyrano as a layered, translated text is the subject of the final section of this Scotnote.

8. 'A NEW VERSE TRANSLATION'

When we discuss Morgan's *Cyrano*, which he described in 1992 as 'a new verse translation', we can, of course, consider it as a stand-alone play in Scots, with its own shape, form, concerns and themes, or we can consider it *as* a translation, an attempt to introduce into the Scottish cultural ecosystem an element that was originally foreign. Morgan was, by the time he came to the French play, an accomplished translator of poetry, and in all his translations he attempted to bring into the target language something of the excitement and energy he perceived in the original. In translating *Cyrano de Bergerac*, as we have seen, he produced a layered text, that is partly original and partly derivative. The play has an extra dimension of meaning for those readers, or those members of the audience, who are familiar with the French original, or indeed with other translations into English. His translated text resonates with earlier and alternative versions.

For a fuller sense of how Morgan approached the French original, the reader is directed to David Kinloch (2004). Here, we will simply look at one speech from the play and consider how Morgan went about the business of refashioning the nineteenth-century text, with its specific cultural allusions, into a stageworthy, contemporary Scots version. In many plays, the central character is first introduced to the audience through the eyes of another character, frequently a minor character. This description acts to prime the members of the audience, who are given their first impression of the character. Cyrano's character is sketched vividly in an early scene, Act 1, Scene 2, by the recurring minor character of the poetry-loving pastry chef, Ragueneau, when he is talking to some of Cyrano's friends. In the French text, the original is as follows:

RAGUENEAU
Certes, je ne crois pas que jamais nous le peigne
Le solennel monsieur Philippe de Champaigne;
Mais bizarre, excessif, extravagant, falot,
Il eût fourni, je pense, à feu Jacques Callot
Le plus fol spadassin à mettre entre ses masques:
Feutre à panache triple et pourpoint à six basques,
Cape que par derrière, avec pompe, l'estoc
Lève, comme une queue insolente de coq,
Plus fier que tous les Artabans dont la Gascogne
Fut et sera toujours l'alme Mère Gigogne,
Il promène, en sa fraise à la Pulcinella,
Un nez! ... Ah! messeigneurs, quel nez que ce nez-là! ...
On ne peut voir passer un pareil nasigère
Sans s'écrier: 'Oh! non, vraiment, il exagère!'
Puis on sourit, on dit: 'Il va l'enlever ...' Mais
Monsieur de Bergerac ne l'enlève jamais.

A line-by-line paraphrase of this speech in standard English prose would be something like this:

RAGUENEAU
For sure, I don't believe that he'll ever be portrayed/By the solemn Monsieur Philippe de Champaigne;/But, weird, excessive, extravagant, unique,/He would have provided, I think, the late Jacques Callot/With the craziest swordsman ever to put on a visor:/With triple plumed hat and six-pointed doublet,/Sword thrusting up under his cape,/Proudly, like an insolent cock's tail,/Prouder than all of the Artabans of Gascony/Who ever were produced by their mother, Gigogne,/He wears above his ruffed Pulcinella collar,/A nose! ... Ah!

Edwin Morgan's *Cyrano de Bergerac* 57

Sirs, what a nose this nose is!/You cannot see such a creature
go by/Without saying, 'Oh! no, really, this is too much!'/
Then we smile, we say, 'He'll take it off ...' But/Monsieur de
Bergerac never takes it off.

Morgan translates this speech as follows (pp. 9–10):

RAGUENEAU
True. An auld fart like Philip of Champaigne
Will niver pent his portrait. Agin the grain!
But auld Emilio Coia, therr's the boay who'd
Huv fixed this heich-skeich wild outlandish dude
Oan a canvas. Yon hat wi its triple plume,
The six-flapped doublet, the cape that swalls back roon,
His stickie-oot sword like a cock's pawky tail,
That gallus Gascon swagger, the niver-fail
Buckle-swash, the birse and brangle, the birkie
Breengein fae a line o birkies, the quirky
Ruff at his neck, sae Punchinello-teuch,
And above that ruff – fellas, it's eneuch
Tae get ye gibberin – a nose, a neb, a niz –
The hooter-bearer passes – 'Cannae be!' 'It is!' –
'It's no. He'll take it aff, jist wait.' They laugh,
But Bergerac will niver take it aff.

Morgan's virtuoso skill in translating into Scots verse the French original text is here apparent. The original speech begins with a reference to two artists of whom Rostand's audience would presumably have been aware: the staid society portraitist, Philippe de Champaigne (1602–1674), and Jacques Callot (1592–1635), a printmaker from Lorraine, who specialised in lively portraits of the low life of his period, the drunks and beggars, as well as the courtly elite. Rostand does not need to explain the relationship between them, but Morgan cannot make the same assumption for his audience. He therefore tells us explicitly what to think of the first artist: 'the auld fart' would find it 'agin the grain' to paint Cyrano's portrait. And then Morgan substitutes for Callot a reference to one of his own contemporaries, the Glasgow-born caricaturist, Emilio Coia, whose illustrations of performers in the Edinburgh International Festival were, at the time of the translation's first production, a prominent feature in the Scotsman newspaper. While dropping Callot, Morgan finds an appropriate and relevant equivalent artist that his own audience will recognise. In this respect he 'domesticates' the Rostand original by bringing it closer to his audience in Scotland.

The rest of the speech finds Morgan conveying in Scots most of the information that is found in Rostand without giving a literal paraphrase. He explains Cyrano's appearance (*'bizarre, excessif, extravagant, falot'* becomes 'heich-skeich wild ootlandish'), and he describes his attire (*'panache triple et pourpoint à six basques'* becomes 'Yon hat wi its triple plume/ The six-flapped doublet'). He makes reference to Cyrano's ancestry ('That gallus Gascon swagger ... Breengein fae a line o birkies') without going into the same level of detail about the family (which can be glossed as 'proudest of the Artabans of Gascony, going back to their proverbial mother, "Mère Gigogne"'). And he makes reference to the prominent facial feature that can be seen above the kind of collar that the stock dramatic character, Punchinello, wears (Morgan again tells us what to think of this detail: 'Punchinello-*teuch*'). That is, he refers to Cyrano's 'nez' ('a nose, a neb, a niz!'). Morgan, in more detail than Rostand, reports the delighted debate amongst those passers-by who see Cyrano's nose ('Cannae be!' 'It is!' 'It's no!' 'He'll take it aff, jist wait!') before delivering the poignant final line, *'Mais/Monsieur de Bergerac ne l'enlève jamais,'* that is, 'But Bergerac will niver take it aff.'

When we look in detail at the French text and the 'new verse translation' of 1992, then, we can see where and how Morgan chooses to parallel Rostand closely, and where he expands, makes a nuance explicit, ramps up the drama, and finds an equivalent expression that will convey the force of the original to an audience separated in time and space from Rostand's first public. The demands of refashioning the French lines into rhyming Scots also become clearer, as does Morgan's skill and invention in rising to this challenge.

Activity

The French text of *Cyrano de Bergerac* is available online, as are several English translations of Rostand's original. Take a relatively short speech or exchange from Morgan's *Cyrano*, and find the equivalent passage in the source text. If your French is good enough, you can compare the two passages directly. If not, then by using translation software, and/or referring to the English translations, explore the ways in which Morgan adapted his source text. Pay attention to his additions and deletions – what does he expand upon, and what does he contract? Does he echo the original closely in places (e.g. by using 'niz' for '*nez*')? Does he make the French original more Scottish, or does he make the Scottish text more French?

If you feel that you would like a challenge, take part of the French original text, or a literal English translation of it, and turn it into Scots. Remember that your lines should have ten syllables (five of which should be stressed) as well as rhyming couplets. Can you sustain this over the length of a play?

9. CONCLUSION

As Edwin Morgan observes in his introduction to the play, cited earlier, *Cyrano* 'is one of those rich and challenging works which need to be translated again and again, in different circumstances and for different purposes, readerly and actorly' (p. xi). Not all translations become significant works of art, in their own right, but Morgan's *Cyrano* shows signs of doing so. As we have noted, originally premiered in 1992, its most recent revival was in 2018, at the Citizens Theatre in Glasgow. The reasons are not hard to see. The play is perennially popular in itself and it remains a fixture of popular culture in the French and English-speaking worlds. It does so because it embodies a particular type of theatricality – it is a heroic tragicomedy that asks its audience to address eternal questions, such as, 'Does art spring from formal ingenuity or sincerity? What is the relationship of the body to the soul? Is love defined as an attraction to the physical body, or the soul, or both? And how should *we* perform the drama of our lives – as our individual code of honour demands, or as corrupt society expects us to? What happens to us when we believe that the only way in which we can be sincere is through deception?'

The way that Rostand addresses these questions makes his *Cyrano* a gift to any translator. However, Morgan took this gift and enhanced it by reinvigorating the source text in a way that honours the spirit of the original: the freshness, ingenuity and dynamism of his Scots verse marks *Cyrano* out as the representative of a new type of aesthetic, one where an idiom based on Glaswegian speech can soar to lyrical heights and plumb comic depths, especially in comparison to the 'Classical' verse that the play regularly mocks. Morgan's translation triumphantly celebrates a too-often stigmatised idiom, and so, for the Scottish audience as much as the French one, *Cyrano* has become a national treasure, characterised, above all, by its *panache*.

10. FURTHER READING

Editions

There is currently one edition of Morgan's *Cyrano*, and it has a brief but insightful introduction by the translator:

Morgan, Edwin (tr.) *Edmond Rostand's Cyrano de Bergerac: A New Verse Translation.* Manchester: Carcanet, 1992.

Various editions of the French original by Edmond Rostand, and other English translations are available in printed form, and online, and they are worth tracking down for comparison. A particularly interesting text to compare with Morgan's is an adaptation in English that updates the setting of the play to 1930s India: Verma, Jatinda and Bolt, Ranjit (trs.) *Cyrano by Edmond Rostand*, Bath: Absolute Classics, 1995.

Secondary Reading

Corbett, J. 'The Summer of Cyrano' *Scottish Literary Review* 4:2, 2012, pp. 145–62 [This article discusses different versions of *Cyrano*.]

Corbett J. *Written in the Language of the Scottish Nation: A History of Literary Translation into Scots.* Clevedon: Multilingual Matters, 1999. [Deals with *Cyrano* briefly in a broader discussion of the literary value of translations into Scots.]

Kinloch, D. 'Edwin Morgan's Cyrano de Bergerac' in B. Findlay, ed. *Frae Ither Tongues: Essays on Modern Translations into Scots.* Clevedon: Multilingual Matters, 2004, pp. 123–44. [An excellent discussion of Morgan's play in the context of its first performance, its themes, and its relationship to the original.]

McGonigal, James. *The Poetry of Edwin Morgan.* ASLS Scotnote No. 2 (2nd edn). Glasgow: Association for Scottish Literary Studies, 2013.

Levinson, S. 'Putting linguistics on a proper footing: Explorations in Goffman's concepts of participation.' In P. Drew and A. Wootton, eds. *Erving Goffman: Exploring the Interaction Order.* Oxford: Polity Press, 1988, pp. 161–227. [For those interested in the concept of 'footing', this is a lucid discussion and critique of Goffman's model of participant roles.]

11. GLOSSARY

This glossary gives English equivalents of words and phrases that might cause difficulty to the reader who is unused to reading Scots, as well as explanations of some ephemeral slang, coinages, a few French borrowings, and technical expressions. I have also explained a number of the references to Classical, French, Scottish and Anglo-American culture, where that seemed necessary or useful. As many of the words in the text are 'phonetic' spellings, the most easily recognisable have been omitted from the glossary, mainly verb forms ending in -in/-it, such as *alternatin* ('alternating'), *attackin* ('attacking'), *distractit* ('distracted'), and some noun forms such as *mornin* ('morning'), etc. Where the stem is also distinctively spelled, however, I have included the word in the glossary, e.g. *cairryin* ('carrying').

Like many writers in Scots, Edwin Morgan did not trouble himself too much with consistency, and so variant spellings are found for particular words, e.g. *foallied, foallowed* ('followed') and the Scots forms often alternate in the text with their English equivalents.

a: reduced form of 'of'
aboot: about
academicianettes: female members of the French academy (see below)
academy, the French: the *Académie française*, formally established by Cardinal Richelieu around 1630 and consisting of the forty most distinguished literary men of France, the so-called 'immortals.' It quickly became the guardian of conservative literary fashion, and codified French vocabulary, grammar and rhetoric
achiacrostopastiche: a compound of *acrostic*, a form of verse in which a set of letters, such as the initial or final letters of each line, spell out a word, and *pastiche*, a work of art in the style or manner of another
ae: of
aff: off
afore: before
aften: often

Edwin Morgan's *Cyrano de Bergerac*

agin: against
Agrippina: a Roman empress, younger sister of Nero, whose death was dramatised by Thomas May (1595–1650) as *The Tragedy of Julia Agrippina, Empress of Rome*
Ah: I
aheid: ahead
ahint: behind
ain: own
aipple: apple
airms: arms
airmy: army
Aladdin: the hero of a Middle-eastern folk tale
alane: alone
alang: along
Alcandre: a female character in Homer's *The Odyssey*
alky: alcoholic, drunkard
aloo: allow
amang: among
Amtrak: company that runs passenger trains in the US
anither: another
anyhin: anything
anti-shabbies: people who are not shabby, i.e. elegant people
Apollo: god of the sun, poetry and music; also known as Phoebus
apricotize: add apricots to
Archytas: Greek philospher (c. 400–365 BCE), reputed to have built a mechanical dove
Aristophanes: Greek comic playwright (c. 446-c. 386 BCE)
aroon: around
atween: between
auld: old
aumond: almond
aw: all
awfy: awful, very
awright: all right
awsorts: all sorts
ay, aye: yes

baa: ball
baack: back
Bacchant, Bacchantes: follower(s) of Bacchus, the Greek god of the wine-harvest, and drunkenness
baith: both
ballade: a verse form consisting of three stanzas of eight lines having an identical rhyme scheme, followed by a four-line stanza. The eight-line stanzas and the four-line stanza all end with the same line
bampot: reckless idiot
bam: reduced version of 'bampot'
banditti: outlaws, robbers
bane: bone. 'baldy-bane': bald-head.
bangster: a ruffian, a bully, a braggart
Bapaume: small town located in northern France.
barbershoap: barber-shop
Baro, Balthazar: French poet and playwright (1596–1650) in the Classical tradition
Barsac: a fine, sweet wine, noted for its refinement, from the Barsac township in France
Barthénoïde: one of the *précieuses*, or seventeenth-century literary women of France, who enjoyed lively conversation and wit
basht: bashed
bassinet: cradle or crib for a new-born infant
bate: beat
battert: battered
bauns: bones; 'sojer-bauns' bones of dead soldiers
baur: humorous incident, or its telling
bawheid: stupid person
baws: balls

beelin: furiously angry
Beelzebub: name for the Devil
bein: being
bel canto: literally, the Italian for 'beautiful song'
Belshazzar: king of Babylon, whose magnificent feast for a thousand lords is the subject of the Book of Daniel, Chapter 5
beltit: belted
ben: inside
Benserade, Isaac de: French poet (1613–1691), member of the Academy
berr: bear, large person
birk: birch tree
birkie: smart young fellow
birse: temper
blate: timid, shy
blatt: incoherent flow of words
blatter: rain storm
blaw: blow
bleck, bleckness: black, blackness
bliddy: bloody
blin: blind
blootered, blootert: drunk
bluid, bluidless,: blood, bloodless
boady: body
boak: throw up, vomit; 'gie wan the boak': make one nauseous
boarn: born
boather, boathersome: bother, bothersome
boattle: bottle
boattom: bottom
boax: box
boay: boy
bod: person; 'bods and sods': variant of 'odds and sods', i.e. a rabble
boke: throw up, vomit; 'gie wan the boke': make one nauseous
bon mot: a clever or witty remark
bonce-jet: head-cracker
bool: ball or rounded object, e.g. a marble

borra: borrow
braid: broad
brambles: blackberries
brammer: attractive person, usually female
brangle: shake, brandish (a weapon)
brangly: proud, swaggering
braw: fine, handsome
breeks: trousers
breenge: charge impetuously
breid: bread
breist: breast
brek: break
brither, britherly: brother, brotherly
broat: brought
Brocken: the highest peak of the Herz mountain range in Saxony, site of a famous optical illusion known as the 'Brocken spectre', caused by the shadows of the spectators being magnified and projected onto the mists of the opposite mountain
broo: brow, forehead
broon: brown
brote: brought
bruit: brute
bubblyjocks: turkey cock
Buckingham, George Villiers, first Duke of: English nobleman (1592–1628) who negotiated the marriage of Prince Charles to Henrietta Maria of France; appears as a character in Dumas' *The Three Musketeers*
buckle-swash: inversion of 'swashbuckle', to show bravado in daring adventures
Bucquoi, Comte de: Charles Bonaventure de Longueval, Count of Bucquoy (1571–1621), a military commander who fought for the Spanish.

bumflin: rolling up, untidily
bummers, heid: bosses, leaders
bummin: bragging, boasting
bunch a fives: punch
bunnet: bonnet, cap
burds: birds
Burgundy, Richelieu, s'il vous plaît: Burgundy, Richelieu, if you please
bushido: sparring; lit. 'the way of the warrior', i.e. the traditional code of the Samurai
byke: beak, nose
byordnar: extraordinary
cacks: excrement, droppings
cadet: a member of the Cadets of Gascony, a French regiment that was mainly recruited from the youngest sons of the aristocratic families of Gascony.
Caesar: Julius Caesar, a Roman general who had an affair with the Egyptian queen, Cleopatra
caird: card
cairdinal: cardinal
cairriage: carriage
cairry: carry
caivalry: cavalry
camshachle: put in disarray, bend, twist
cannae: can't
canto: see *bel canto*
cantrips: antics, mischief
caparisons: soldier's equipment
Capuchin: Franciscan friar, distinguished by his pointed hood
carin: caring
caterans: Highland marauders
cattle-marra: beef marrow fat
cauf: calf of leg
cauld: cold
caunle: candle
caw: call
chairge: charge
chancer: opportunist
chancy: unreliable
chanty: chamber-pot
chanty wrassler: idle boaster
chap: knock, strike or stamp
Chapelain, Jean: French man of letters (1595–1674), founder member of the Académie française, who conceived the idea of a dictionary of the French language
chaw: chew
cherm, chermer: charm, charmer
cherr: chair
chestnits: chestnuts
chevalier: French title, equivalent to the English 'knight'
chevron: a v-shaped sign on a heraldic shield or 'escutcheon', signifying protection
chimley: chimney
chitterin-fit: fit of shivering
chuckies: small pebbles
chynge: change
cicadas: insects that make a loud droning sound by vibrating membranes on their abdomen
Cid, The: Rodrigo Díaz de Vivar (c. 1043–1099), a Castilian nobleman and military leader in medieval Spain. The Moors called him 'El Cid' or 'The Cid'. Many works of literature and drama have been based on his life, including a play by Corneille, *Le Cid* (1636).
clachan: village
claes: clothes
clairty: dirty
clan: local or family group
cleek: catch, hook or ensnare
Cleopatra: Egyptian queen who had an affair with the Roman general, Julius Caesar

cloack: clock
cloagged: clogged
cloke: clock
clouts: hits on and around the head
c'moan: come on
coallar: collar
coamet: comet
coamic: comic
coansciousness: consciousness
coarner: corner
coatton: cotton
cobs: round loaves
Coia, Emilio: Glasgow-born caricaturist (1911–1997) whose portraits of performers in the Edinburgh International Festival appeared in the *Scotsman*
combobulate: make smooth and pleasant (the antonym of *discombobulate*: upset or confuse)
commedia: *commedia dell'arte*, a form of comic theatre, originating in Italy, that was popular throughout Europe from the sixteenth to the eighteenth centuries. The characters are usually stereotypical, stock characters
comte: the French form of the title of 'count'
coofs: fool, incompetent person, rogue
coont: count
coop, cart; to cowp the coops: lit. to overturn the cart, fig. to spend a lot of money
coorie: bend, crouch
coorse: coarse, vulgar
coort: court; **coortin:** wooing
Copernicus, Nicolas: mathematician and astronomer (1473–1543) who proposed that the Sun, not the Earth, is the centre of the universe
coquettes: women who enjoy flirting
Corneille, Pierre: French playwright (1606–1684), author of such plays as *Le Cid*
corrieneuchin: conversing intimately
coudnae, couldnae: couldn't
cowp, to overturn; **to cowp the coops:** lit. to overturn the cart, fig. to spend a lot of money
crack: talk, gossip, conversation
cratur: creature
craw: crow
cric crac!: meaningless exclamation
crits: reduced form of 'criticisms', i.e. reviews of a performance
croass: cross, angry
crockanition: smithereens
cronies: friends, bosom pals (from the Greek *chronios*, long-continued)
croon: crown
croose: cheerful, merry
crummlin: crumbling
cry: call, name
cud: could
cundy: covered drain
Cupid: god of love, equipped with bow, arrows and a torch with which to inflame the hearts of lovers
currish: like a cur, or dog
da: familiar name for father, or old man
dab: 'to let dab' to disclose information, usually in the negative, 'no let dab'
dae: do
daffin: playing
daft: foolish
daith: death
dammit: damn it

dapped: dropped gently into, dipped
D'Artagnan, Charles de Baatz: a famous guardsman, whose exploits are the subject of Alexandre Dumas' *The Three Musketeers*
D'Assoucy, Charles Coypeau: French poet and musician (1605–1677)
dauner: stroll, short walk
dauphin: title given to the heir to the throne of France
daur: dare
daurk, daurkest/daurkist: dark, darkest
deave: deafen, annoy with loud chatter
dee: die, do
deef: deaf
deid: dead
deil: devil
demisemiquaver: a musical note played for 1/32 of the duration of a whole note
denner: dinner
derrière: behind
Descartes, René: French rationalist philosopher (1596–1650)
Diana: Roman goddess of the hunt, associated with chastity
dibble: plant
dicht: wipe, dress a wound
didnae: didn't
dinna, dinnae: don't
dirdums: uproar, noise
disnae: doesn't
dither: hesitate
divil: devil
divnae: don't
doacter, doactor: doctor
dod: a piece of something taken from a larger quantity
doe's fud: the buttocks of a doe, a female deer
doh, high: a state of agitated excitement
donnart: dull, stupid
Don Quixote: a novel by Miguel de Cervantes Saavedra published in two parts (1605 & 1615), featuring a deluded knight who in one episode attacks windmills, believing they are giants
doo: dove, pigeon
doon: down
doonbeat: downbeat
doongradit: downgraded
doot: doubt, suspect
doucely: sedately, sweetly
drap, draplet: drop, droplet
drooly: salivating
drouth: thirst
duffer: old fool
dug: dog
dumpling: fool
dunk: dip into a drink or soup
dunt: knock forcefully
durt, durty: dirt, dirty
dwam: faint, stupor, daydream
easy oasy: easy-going, lazy
eejit: idiot
eftir: after
eneuch: enough
Englan: England
Epy: L'Epy or L'Espy (The Spy) was the stage name of an actor in Molière's company
erm: arm
ermy: army
erse: arse
escutcheon: a shield-shaped, heraldic emblem
Esmeraldesque: like Esmerelda, the beautiful gypsy heroine of Victor Hugo's The *Hunchback of Notre Dame*
euphuistic: an excessively sophisticated literary style of the late 1500s and early 1600s

eyebroos: eyebrows
fa: who
fae: from
faithful: faithful
faldelal: playful foolishness
fantoosh: flashy, the height of fashion
fareweel: farewell
fauld: fold
faur: far
faw: fall
feart, feartie/fearty: frightened; a frightened person
fecht, fechter: fight; fighter
feenish: finish
feint: divert attention from true purpose
fella: fellow
fermer: farmer
fidgin-fain: restlessly excited
fikey: fussy, difficult to handle
fin: find
finicky: fussy, over-elaborate
firget: forget
firkin: small wooden barrel
fistula: abnormal opening or channel between two organs; pipe through which at one time the Pope took consecrated wine
fit: foot
fitmen: footmen
flair: floor
Flanders: the Dutch-speaking northern part of Belgium
flang: flung
flee: fly, escape from
flerr: floor
flit, dae a: move from one home, or place, to another
floappy: floppy
flooer, flooery: flower, flowery
Flugga: see *Muckle Flugga*
foallae, foally: follow
foarests: forests

Fontainebleau: site of a magnificent sixteenth-century French royal palace
forbye: besides
forgie: forgive
forgote: forgot
forloarn: forlorn
fower, fowr: four
freen, freenless, freenship: friend; friendless; friendship
freneticate: become frenzied
Freuchie: a village in Fife, by the royal Falkland Palace
fribble: trifler
fricht: fright
fu: full, drunk
fud: the buttocks or tail of an animal, female pubic hair or sexual organs
fulla: full of
funambulist: tightrope performer
fur: for
furrish: very furry
furrit: forward
furst: first
fykes: vocal fussiness, commotions
gabby: talkative
gaed: went
gaird: guard
gairden: garden
gairdsman: guardsman
galantine: dish of veal, chicken or other white meat, boned, minced, tied up, boiled, and then served cold
Galileo, Galilei: Italian astronomer and mathematician (1564–1642)
gallus: bold, cocky, strutting, flashy – in the west of Scotland, frequently a compliment
galoot: foolish person, often tall
Gascon: a native of Gascony, a region of southwest France

Edwin Morgan's *Cyrano de Bergerac*

Gassendi, Pierre: French philosopher and mathematician (1596–1655) who tutored Molière; Gassendi-san: address using Gassendi's name plus the Japanese honorific *–san,* 'sir'
Gassion, Jean, Comte de: a Gascon military commander (1609–1647)
gaun: going
gawdsagawds: comical oath
gawdsdeddo: comical oath
gawdsgawb: comical oath, 'God's mouth'
gawdspapawl: comical oath
gawdstoptop: comical exclamation
geddit: get it
Genoa: Italian city
gett: brat
gey: very, considerably
gie: give
ginger: soft, carbonated drink
gingerbreid, gingerbried: gingerbread
girn: moan, compain
girner: moaner
glaury: muddy
gled: glad
glen: valley
gless: glass
glisk: gleam, sparkle, flash
gloaming: twilight, dusk
globefu: globefull
Goadsboady: oath, 'God's body'
goannae, goanny, goany: going to
Gode: God
Godesake: oath, 'God's sake'
Godestruth: oath, 'God's truth'
Godzilla: giant mutant reptile in Japanese and American science fiction films
goffer: crimp, impress a pattern in lace
gonnae, gonny: going to

Gorgon: creature in Greek myths capable of turning whoever sees her into stone
gote: got
Grammont, Antoine II, Duke of: French military officer and diplomat (1604–1678). Also known as De Guiche, he is, initially, the villain of the play
Grampian: mountainous region of Scotland
gran: grand
greet: weep
gress: grass
gresshopper: grasshopper
gret, gretness: great; greatness
Grizel: short form of the female name 'Griselda'
grot: grotto or cave, dark place
grun: ground
grup: grip
Gucci: an Italian fashion brand, particularly known for leather goods such as shoes
guff: smell, whiff
guid: good
guidsakes: mild oath, 'God's sakes'
gunpouther: gunpowder
guttit: gutted, devastated
hackit: foolish, stupid
hae: have
hail: whole
halesome: wholesome
haly: holy
hame, hamely, hamesick: home; homely; homesick
hanky panky: sexual mischief
***hara kiri*:** Japanese ritual suicide by disembowelment
hasnae: hasn't
hauden: held
hauf: half
haunle: handle
haun: hand
haurd, haurdly: hard; hardly

heeze: lift, elevate
heich-skeich: high-spirited
heid: head
heidscarf: headscarf
Helen: a beautiful Greek woman whose abduction sparked the Trojan War; in Homer's *Iliad*, she goes willingly with her captor
hemistich: a half-line of verse
hems: a horse's collar; 'pit the hems oan', keep in order, curb
hen: familiar term of address for a female, esp. a young woman
Henry the Fourth: the first Bourbon king of France (1553–1610)
Hercules: Roman hero and god, known for his great strength
herm, hermless: harm, harmless
herr: hair
hersel: herself
hert: heart
hidalgo: Spanish gentleman of noble descent
himsel: himself
hingin: hanging
hing: thing
hinnie: honey, sweetheart; term of endearment
hippocampelelephantocamelou: an imaginary creature living on the moon
hisnae: hasn't
hivtae: have to
hiz: has
hoaliday: holiday
hoarn: horn
hoarse: horse
hoat: hot
hod: hold
hon: hand
honkered: nosed
hoo: how
hoolet: owl
hoose: house
Hornblower, Horatio: courageous but sensitive hero of a series of historical nautical novels by C. S. Forester (1899–1966)
hote: hot
howzit: how is it
huckles: hips, haunches
hud: had
humph: lift or carry a heavy burden
hunner: hundred
hup: exclamation
hure: whore, prostitute
huv: have
hypermacho: excessively masculine in manner
icosahedron: a twenty-sided solid
Iliad: Greek epic poem by Homer about the Greek-Trojan war
infantine: infantile, childish
inflatit: inflated
insteeda: instead of
intae: into
Ithaca: home of Ulysses and Penelope, in Homer's epic poems
ither: other
itsel: itself
iv: of
iver: ever
ivry: every
ivrythin, ivrything: everything
ivrywan: everyone
ivrywhere: everywhere
iz: reduced form of 'his'
ivy-bine: climbing tendril of ivy
janny: reduced form of 'janitor', the caretaker of a public building
jinky: with quick and nimble movements
jist: just
joab: job
joco: merry, pleased with oneself

Jodelet: a famous stage actress
John of Austria: military leader (1547–1578) in the service of Spain
jougs: an instrument of public punishment: a hinged and locked collar, fastened by a chain to a wall or post
jouk: dodge, avoid
joukerie pokerie: trickery, deceit
jujube: a gelatin lozenge, tasting of the jujube berry
Juliet: the young female lover in Shakespeare's *Romeo and Juliet*
jyne: join
jynin: joining
kaput: finished, over
kebab: skewering
keekin: peeping
keelie: rough, urban, working-class male, often associated with criminality
kent: knew
kerve: carve
keys, tae cry: to call a truce, as in a playground game of tag
kilt: killed
kin: can
kina: can't
kist: chest
knoack: knock
kulchur: culture (the spelling echoes Ezra Pound's *Guide to Kulchur*, 1938)
laird: lord, rank given to the owner of landed property or an estate
lanelie: lonely
lang, langer: long; longer
lang whang: long strip of leather; Lang Whang: a stretch of the old Edinburgh–Lanark road
Lanliq: brand of cheap sherry, popular in certain quarters of Glasgow

lawlander: lowlander
Lazarus: Biblical character, raised from the dead by Christ
lea: leave
leal: loyal
lee, leear: lie, falsehood; liar
len: lend
licht, lichtsome: light; cheerful
loada: load of
loass: loss
loast: lost
loat: lot
loata: lot of
loch: lake
loon: lad, young farm-worker, fellow
Lothario: handsome male character in Nicholas Rowe's *The Fair Penitent* (1703), notorious for having many lovers
lotsa: lots of
loup: leap
lud: lord, in *m'lud*, 'my lord'
lug: ear
lukkin: looking
lum: chimney
Lysimon: possibly the character called Demea in the Roman playwright Terence's *Adelphi – the Brothers*, sometimes rechristened 'Lysimon' in later translations
ma: my
macaroons: small biscuits, typically made from ground nuts with a sweet filling and chocolate coating
madeleine: light sponge cake
Maecenas, Gaius Cilnius: celebrated Roman patron of young writers (d. 8 BCE)
mair: more
mairriage: marriage
maist: most
maitter, maitters: matter; matters

Malherbe, François de: French poet, critic and translator (1556–1628), credited with developing the restraint and poetic techniques associated with Classicism

Mancini, La: one of five nieces of Cardinal Mazarin who, around 1650, attended the court of King Louis XIV in the hope of finding a suitable husband. The sisters were known as the *Mazarinettes*

manky: dirty

marra: marrow

masel: myself

mauvais quart d'heure: bad quarter of an hour

mell: concern oneself improperly with, mingle, mix

mensefu: well-mannered, polite

merit: married

mibbe: maybe

mick, take the: make fun of

midden: refuse heap, dunghill, dustbin; 'tae the middens': to the furthest border of one's property

mind: remember

mither: mother

moadest, moadesty: modest; modesty

moarnin, moarning: morning

molocate: beat to a pulp

moniplies: a small container; literally, the third stomach of a ruminant

La Montglat: Jeanne de Harlay (1580–1643), French court official and daughter of Baron de Montglat

mony: many

mooth: mouth

morituri: those who are about to die

morra, the: tomorrow

Morvern: area in the north-west Highlands of Scotland

muckle, Muckle Flugga: large, great; the most northerly of a rocky outcrop in the sea, north of the Shetland Islands

muin: moon

muinlicht: moonlight

mulk, Mulky Way: milk; Milky Way, a band of light across the night sky, caused by billions of stars

Munich tankard: large beer mug

Murdoch, Rupert: an Australian businessman and media tycoon, proprietor of an international network of newspapers and television channels, such as *The Times*, the *Sun*, Sky and Fox; 'Murdoch Shturdoch': expression of disdain or contempt

muscat, muscatel: sweet white wine from the muscat grape

musta: must have

na, nae: not, no

naebdy: nobody

naethin: nothing

nane: none

narg it: grumble continuously

naw: no

neb: nose

neebors: neighbours

neednae: needn't

neep: turnip

nevvy: nephew

ninny: fool

nippit: inhibited, constricted

niver, nivir: never

nixt: next

niz: nose

Edwin Morgan's *Cyrano de Bergerac* 75

noo: now
nuhhin: nothing
nummer: number
nut: emphatic 'not'
nuthin: nothing
nyaff: insignificant little person
o: of
oan: on
oasy: see *easy oasy*
ony: any
onywey: anyway
oor: our; hour
oot, oota: out; out of
Orpheus: in Greek mythology, a gifted musician who failed to recover his wife, Eurydice from the underworld. Later, he was torn to pieces by a group of jealous Thracian women
ower: over
pair, pair sowl: poor; poor soul
pairt: part
pairtrick: partridge
panky: see *hanky panky*
pash: break into small pieces
patter: fluent, witty banter
paurdon: pardon
pavane: music for a stately sixteenth-century costume dance
pawky: roguish, sly
pech: pant, puff
Penelope: faithful wife of Ulysses in Homer's epic poem, *The Odyssey*; in her husband's absence she promised her suitors she would remarry after she had finished weaving a shroud, but each night she unravelled what she had woven during the day
pentit: painted
perfick: perfect
perr, perra: pair; pair of

Perrier: a brand of mineral water
petitpoint: a type of stitch in embroidery
petits fours: small, bite-sized appetiser or confectionery
pey: pay
peymaister: paymaster
Phaedo: the main character in Balthazar Baro's tragi-comedy, *Clorise*
Philip of Champaigne: Philippe de Champaigne, a French baroque artist (1602–1674), one of the founders of the French academy of painting and sculpture
Phoebus: god of the sun, poetry and music; also known as Apollo
photy: photograph
Phyllis: a shepherdess, the subject of a sonnet sequence by Thomas Lodge (1558–1625)
pinkie: little finger
pit: put
pley: play
plook: pimple, boil; term of abuse for someone
ploy: enterprise; practical joke
plume: tuft of feathers on a hat or helmet; in French, *panache*
plunk: fall with a dull, heavy sound
poakit: pocket
poassible: possible
poaverty: poverty
pokerie: see *joukerie pokerie*
poo: bad smell
pooer: power
popcoarn: popcorn
popinjay: vain or conceited person; parrot
pree: experience; test by trying out
prink: strut, swagger
prood: proud
puir: poor

Punch, Punchinello: originally 'Pulcinello', the dim-witted servant in *commedia dell'arte* plays, who evolved into the hook-nosed, ill-tempered wife-murderer of 'Punch and Judy' puppet shows
pynt: point
Pyramus: a character whose tragic love affair with Thisbe is retold in various poems and plays, and parodied in Shakespeare's *A Midsummer Night's Dream*
pyson: poison
quack: unqualified doctor
Quixote: see *Don Quixote*
radgie: excited, keen, crazy
raither: rather
Rambo: John Rambo, muscular hero of American action films, portrayed by Sylvester Stallone
recaw: recall
Regiomontanus: pseudonym of Johannes Müller (1436–1476), German astronomer and mathematician, reputed to have designed a wooden eagle capable of flying
rerr: rare; wonderful
respeck, respeckfu: respect; respectful
Richelieu, Cardinal: French statesman (1585–1642), patron of the arts and founder of the French Academy
richt: right
rid: red
ridicuckoldous: insertion of the word 'cuckold', a husband whose wife is adulterous, into the word 'ridiculous'
rien: nothing
romanzas: romances, fanciful stories

Romeo: ill-fated male lover in Shakespeare's play, *Romeo and Juliet*
roon: round
Rotrou, Jean de: French playwright (1609–1650)
Rouen: French port city, capital of Normandy
rowp: auction
ruderie: vulgarity
rudester: insolent fellow
rummle: rumble
sae: so
Saint-Amant: Antoine Girard, sieur de Saint-Amant (1594–1661), French poet
saft, saften: soft; soften
saip: soap
sair: sore, sorely; great, greatly
saltpetre: chemical compound used in fertilisers and fireworks
Samson: Biblical hero, known for his great strength
saumon: salmon
sayed: said
Scapin: the protagonist of Molière's *Les Fourberies de Scapin* (1671), based on the stock character of Scapino, a roguish servant familiar in Italian comedy
scart: scratch
sclim: climb
scoarched: scorched
Scoatch: Scots
scoonrel: scoundrel
scrunty: shrivelled, shrunken
scud: glide swiftly
scunner, scunnersome: feel disgust; something that prompts the feeling of disgust
scutard: someone who defecates
sedulous: showing dedication and diligence
seek: sick
Seine: river flowing through Paris

Edwin Morgan's *Cyrano de Bergerac* 77

sel: self
senna: leaf of the cassia plant
seraphim: one of the highest order of angels
Setterday: Saturday
shadda: shadow
shair: sure
shairly: surely
shamefu: shameful
shaw: show
shedda: shadow
sherp: sharp
shillelagh: Irish wooden walking stick or cudgel
shoap: shop
shoart: short
shoat: shot
shoo: a cry used to scare away
shoulda: should have
shouldnae: shouldn't
shouther: shoulder
shtick: preference; performance that follows a familiar pattern
sic, sich: such
sidieweys: sideways
Sidney, Sir Philip: English poet (1554–1586), author of a sequence of love sonnets
siller: silver, cash
Sirius: bright star, known as the Dog Star
skeely: skilful
skeich: high-spirited, daft, skittish
skein: a quantity of thread or yarn, wound into a loose knot
skelf: splinter, fragment
skelp: strike, hit; move quickly
skirlin: shrill sound, wailing
skiver: layabout, someone who avoids work
skliff: swipe in passing; shuffle
slaisterin: splashing, smearing
slanty: descending in height
slaw: slow
slicerama: machine for slicing up meat (coinage)
slorpin: slurping
slutettes: females with loose morals
smeek: fumes, smoke (North-east Scots)
smert: smart
smoother: smother, choke
snaffle: snatch
snaw: snow
sneck: latch, fasten
snick: catch, seize, steal
snubby: snub-nosed
snuff, snuffle: sniff
snuffler: someone who sniffs
soacks: socks
Socrates: Greek philosopher (469–399 BCE)
sojer: soldier
somebdy: somebody
somewan: someone
sook, sook up tae: suck; ingratiate oneself with
soomin: swimming
soond: sound
soople: supple
sowl: soul, person
sozzled: drunk
Spainish: Spanish
speerit: spirit
sperd: spared
sploke: ejaculation
spoat: spot
sprachled: sprawled out, floundering
spreed: spreak
squerr: square
stane: stone
stank: drain, drainage ditch
stap: stop
stapple: bung, plug, stopper
steamboats: very drunk
steamer: moment of bliss
steir: stir, motivate
sterrs: stairs
stert: start
sterve: starve

stey: stay
stickie-oot: protruding
stieve: firm, stout
stoakins: stockings
stoap: stop
stocious: drunken
ston: stand
stookie: slow-witted, dull person
stooks: stalks
stowp: drinking vessel
straft: strafed, heavily bombarded
strathspey: tune for a Scottish dance, slower than a reel
stravaig: wander
streetch: stretch
sumhm: something
sunbrunt: sunburned
supergun: long-range missile launcher with elongated barrel, whose threatened use by Iraq was widely publicised in the Gulf War of January–February 1991
supersnack: hurry up, come to the point
swall: swell
swatch: array
sweein: swaying
sweer: swear
swish: make a gesture with a rustling sound
swizz: deception
syne: wash, rinse out
'tache: reduced form of 'moustache'
tae: to
taen: taken
taipestry: tapestry
tait: small amount
tap, tapmaist: top; topmost
tarnation: damnation
Taurus: constellation of stars in the shape of a bull
tenshun: reduced form of the command, 'attention'
terr: tear

tertlet: tartlet
teuch: tough
teuchter: uncouth rustic; disparaging name for a northerner, especially a Highland Gaelic speaker
thae: those
thaim: them
thankye: thank you
thay: they
theayter: affected pronunciation of 'theatre', with the stress on 'ay'
thegither: together
theirsels: themselves
therr: there
thimmle: thimble
thon: that
thoosans: thousands
thote: thought
thrang: busy; on friendly terms
thrawn: stubborn
thumscrews: thumbscrews
tirr: bad temper
Titian: Tiziano Vecellio or Veccelli (1488–1576), a renowned Italian artist of the Venetian School
tizz: busy, distracted state
tod, on one's: alone
toke: large hand-rolled cigarette, often containing marijuana
toon: town
tootsies: feet
torte: tart
toty: tiny
Touraine: an old province of France, its capital being Tours
traigedy: tragedy
traivel: travel
trimmle: tremble
triolet: a stanza of eight lines, composed so that the first line rhymes with the fourth and seventh, and the second line rhymes with the eighth

trousseau: clothes and other belongings, collected by a bride-to-be for her wedding
trummles: trembles
tuim: empty
twinty: twenty
Ulysses: the Roman name for the hero of Homer's epic poem, *The Odyssey*
unbumfled: unruffled
unner, unnerneath: under; underneath
unnerston: understand
ur: are
Urimédonte: one of the *précieuses*, or seventeenth-century literary women of France, who enjoyed lively conversation and wit
urny: aren't
uz: us
Valentino, Rudolph: star of silent films (1895–1926), famous for playing romantic roles
vamoose: clear off
Venus: goddess of love
virr: vigour, energy
vous: you
wabbit: feeble, exhausted
wae: with
waff: wave
wahnt: want
wame: stomach
wan, wance: one; once
wanna, wanny: one of
wark: work
warld: world
warst: worst
watter: water
waur: worse
weans: children
wechty: weighty
wee: little
weel: well
weer: wear, tolerate
weet: wet
wemen: women
Wensday: Wednesday
wernae: weren't
wersh: tasteless, insipid; bitter, sour
wey: way
whae: who
whang: thick slice, especially of cheese; see also *Lang Whang*
whase: whose
whatanever, whativer: whatever
whaur: where
wheech: move speedily, whizz
wheen: a few
wheesht: shush, be silent
whigmaleeries: fanciful notions
whiles: sometimes; at other times
whit: what
whummlin: overwhelming
whusslin: whistling
wi: with
wid: would; wood
widda: would have; widow
widen: wooden
widnae: wouldn't
wids: woods
willies, gie the: frighten, upset
wilnae: won't
windae: window
winna: won't
wis: was
wisnae: wasn't
withoot: without
wiz: was
wrang: wrong
wrasslers: wrestlers; see also *chanty wrasslers*
wumman: woman
wunner, wunnerful: wonder; wonderful
wunst: once
wur: our
wurd: word
wurk: work
wurld: world

wurm: worm
wurthiest: worthiest
ya: you
yaird: yard
yaise: use
yalla: yellow
yeese: you (plural)
yella: yellow
yer, yersel: your; yourself
yese: you (plural)
yin: one
yit: yet

yon: that
yuppie: young adult with high earnings who spends them on luxury consumer goods (from 'young upwardly-mobile professional')
zat: reduced form of 'is that'
zen: Eastern philosophy characterised by meditation and a peaceful state of mind
zephyr: soft, gentle breeze from the west

12. APPENDIX

When the late Bill Findlay and I were thinking of including the Scots version of *Cyrano de Bergerac* in an anthology of plays in Scots translation, eventually published as *Serving Twa Maisters*, Edwin Morgan kindly allowed us to consult his personal copy of the 1992 Carcanet edition of his play (signed "Edwin Morgan 23-10-1992") where he had marked up some typographical errors. We also noticed a few more. When we reluctantly decided against including the play in our anthology, I listed the typos as an appendix to my article 'The Summer of Cyrano' in *Scottish Literary Review* 4:2, 2012, pp. 145-62. It might be convenient to reproduce that list here. The page references are to the 1992 edition, and what follows the symbol > is the corrected reading. Morgan identified the following typos:

p. 10, LIGNIÈRE's 2nd speech: Magdaleine > Magdeleine
p. 16, THE CROWD's 1st speech: Monfleury > Montfleury
p. 17, THE CROWD's 2nd speech: Monfleury > Montfleury
p. 24, CYRANO's 3rd speech, line 17: awe > aw
p. 24, CYRANO's 3rd speech, line 23:
    Hippocamelelephantocamelou > Hippocampelephantocamelou
p. 27, VALVERT's 2nd speech: Move line to right
p. 29, A MUSKETEER, line 2: Judge > judge
p. 36, CYRANO's 6th speech: Move line to right
p. 39, 4th speech: OURTH ASTRYCOOK > FOURTH
    PASTRYCOOK
p. 45, FIRST POET's 4th speech, line 1: gingerbrieds >
    gingerbreids
p. 60, DE GUICHE's 5th speech: Your > You
p. 63, line 7: Insert comma after 'hassle'
p. 63, line 15: jourkerie > joukerie

p. 63, line 19: Insert comma after 'Dream'
p. 64, CYRANO's 2nd speech, line 12: an > in
p. 66, LE BRET/CARBON's 1st speech, line 2: teuchers > teuchters
p. 66, CYRANO's 1st speech, line 7: daurkist > darkest
p. 67, CYRANO's 3rd speech, line 2: can > oan
p. 81, DE GUICHE's 3rd speech: Pleas > Please!
p. 92, CYRANO's 2nd speech, line 1: as > aw
p. 108, LE BRET/CARBON's 1st speech, line 2: stervin > servin
p. 125, ROXANE's 4th speech: bet > bit
p. 146, 8th speech: MOTHER MAREURITE > MOTHER MARGUERITE
p. 146, MOTHER MARGUERITE's 5th speech, line 2: Magdaleine > Magdeleine
p. 154, CYRANO's 4th speech, line 4: a fall > fall (i.e. deleted 'a')
p. 157, ROXANE's last speech, line 1: as > aw
p. 161, line 2: love's > lover's

Bill and I identified a few other typographical errors in the 1992 edition. These are as follows:

p. 62, CYRANO's 5th speech, line 4: gummmy > gummy
p. 104, CYRANO's 4th speech, line 2: catttle-marra > cattle-marra
p. 109, CYRANO's 3rd speech, line 2: seee > see
p. 113, CYRANO's 2nd speech, line 8: sleeepy > sleepy
p. 113, CYRANO's 2nd speech, line 23: greeen > green
p. 149, THE DUKE's 2nd speech, line 3: One > one
p. 151, LE BRET/CARBON's 4th speech, line 2: doacter > doactor ('doactor' is the form used elsewhere, including in LE BRET/CARBON's immediately previous speech)
p. 159, ROXANE's 2nd speech, line 2: thay > they ('they' is the form used elsewhere)